Fighting Demons
WHILE CHASING
GOD!

Kimberly Faith Cagle MSEd

ISBN 979-8-89043-318-3 (paperback)
ISBN 979-8-89043-319-0 (digital)

Copyright © 2024 by Kimberly Faith Cagle MSEd

All rights reserved. No part of this publication may be reproduced, distributed, or transmitted in any form or by any means, including photocopying, recording, or other electronic or mechanical methods without the prior written permission of the publisher. For permission requests, solicit the publisher via the address below.

Christian Faith Publishing
832 Park Avenue
Meadville, PA 16335
www.christianfaithpublishing.com

Printed in the United States of America

This book is dedicated to my Lord and Savior, for the courage, strength, and guidance of sharing my story with a lost world so that they may see evidence of his Love, Mercy, Grace, and Forgiveness, but most of all his Salvation.

Also, to my precious husband, who was a wonderful gift sent by God. You are so wonderful and have given me the utmost support and encouragement through our twenty-four years together and have brought me out of despairing circumstances and led me back to our Loving God. I am so honored and blessed to have such a wonderful husband as you.

PREFACE

Reflecting over various occurrences in my life, many would wonder how she is still standing; how am I maintaining a positive outlook? Trust me, I have often asked myself that very same question. The only answer that I give myself and those that ask is: simply God! Like so many others, I realized that the trials and hardships I have faced in my life mirrored what other people had experienced.

Obstacles, trials, emotional, spiritual, and physical battles come in many different forms for everyone. Mine, however, stemmed from the expectation of responsibility for myself and others by the age of nine, growing up alone, death crossing my doorstep so many times that it became second nature to me; so much so I find it difficult to react in a way that would present true mourning. At this point, as if it wasn't already personal enough, let's add early twenties mental breakdowns, autoimmune diagnosis in my early thirties, fighting for my life, career transitions, educational setbacks; basically, questions my very purpose at every turn. To those that do not believe in Christ or God, you may think this is just a bit or a lot of bad luck; however, for those that know Jesus Christ as your Savior, you may consider this a testing of my faith. As I delve deeper into my circumstances, and God's Word, He began to show me that these demons I have been fighting were actually sent directly to me in an effort to curb or steer me away from what I have been called to by my Lord Jesus Christ. Then I began to understand that we are all called for a purpose. I felt that helping others tell their story in a way that would reveal the pain and trauma and the healing that God grants us would be almost therapeutic. That is why I chose to tell Caroline's story. She and I have been working through many obstacles for years. Finding a kindred spirit to share the pain, burdens, and trauma, as well as the healing process, are the angels among us whom God sends.

We all have our demons we face. We all endure a variety of trauma, all of which mold us into who we are. However, not all know the love, grace, and mercy of our Savior. It is not simply an acknowledgment of His presence but a faithful, overpouring relationship with a being who offers the purest and most true love. My mission with this book is to deliver the knowledge I have acquired over the years to others, so they may draw closer to the Lord and find that sincere relationship with Him that will help them face their demons while finding hope in eternity with Jesus Christ in the process.

CHAPTER 1

Prior to My Relationship

For you formed my inward parts; you knitted me together in my mother's womb. I praise you, for I am fearfully and wonderfully made. Wonderful are your works; my soul knows it very well. My frame was not hidden from you, when I was made in secret, intricately woven in the depths of the earth. Your eyes saw my unformed substance; in your book were written, every one of them, the days that were formed for me, when you yet there were none of them.

—Psalm 139:13–16 (ESV)

It is breathtaking to imagine how each of us ultimately came to be with these very thoughts, love, and preparation from our heavenly Father.

Caroline Rose Helton's story began when she was born to a humble tobacco-farming family in a small town near Stokes County, North Carolina. Her mother worked in the office of a copper production company. Her father worked tirelessly at three dramatically different jobs: first shift, as a mechanic at the Bill Hanks Lumber Company; afternoon, he was found farming and raising tobacco and cattle; and third shift, as a mechanic at the same copper production company where her mother worked. Caroline was the baby of the family with one brother, three years older, Oscar. Before starting school, Oscar and Caroline stayed with her father's mom. They called her granny. She was the best at everything, from cooking to showing her love for the kids in a "tough love" fashion. Even though she did not like to say it, you never had to question that she loved you. She never allowed a doubt in anyone's mind of how proud she was of her children, grandchildren, and great-grandchildren. She would boast about any of them in any room to anyone with ears to hear, and she thoroughly enjoyed receiving brags for her contribution to the "raising of such smart, grand, and successful people." But really, do you know any Granny who does not want a bit of credit? She was a God-fearing woman who took pride in raising and teaching Caroline and her cousins. All were held accountable for their actions and were taught honesty, integrity, complex work ethics, and manners (yes, as Caroline is from the South; manners are a must).

Even in such a wonderful family, Caroline explained that she always felt set apart. This is something that Caroline and I have in common and discussed often. For Caroline, the future demons and trials increased her feeling of being set apart. Neither of us could adequately describe those early memories except to explain that she and I felt like outsiders. I am sure that Caroline and I are not the only ones who thought they didn't fit in or were an outsider. Some of the same conversations that Caroline and I have had would cause memories to resurface in many others. With so many diverse disorders recognized today, I often wonder and even suggested to Caroline that I sometimes feel I could be on the spectrum of some sort of irregularity. I am viewing the world differently. Caroline was quick to point out that this overwhelming feeling of being different could also be God's way of preparing and cultivating my heart, mind, and soul, fortifying me to face the obstacles, trials, and demons of the future that is helping me to carry out His will for my life. It is fantastic to have those loved ones, friends, and family in your life to share a bit of Godly insight. In the book of Isaiah, Isaiah tells the story of the chosen servant in a way that should inspire everyone to desire the call of God in their lives.

FIGHTING DEMONS WHILE CHASING GOD!

> *He will not grow faint or be discouraged till he has established justice in the earth; and the coastlands wait for the law. (Isaiah 42:4 ESV)*

> *I am the Lord, I have called you in righteous; I will take you by the hand and keep you; I will give you a covenant for the people a light for the nations. (Isaiah 42:6 ESV)*

First John 1:5 declares God is the light. Our relationship with God demands we have the indwelling Holy Spirit, the third deity of God, and His light within us to live apart, yet within the world, to help shine God's light and guide the world to Christ Jesus, our King and Savior. *Matthew 5:14 tells us that we are "the light of the world, a city set on a hill that cannot be hidden."* Throughout Caroline's childhood, she never imagined those precious thoughts and days God had already written for her would include being called by Him, much less what that preparation for the call looked like beginning at such a young age. Perhaps that distant and set-apart feeling of indifference was the first indication that God had already started to tenderize and cultivate her heart toward His.

Kindergarten was a joyous yet devastating time in Caroline's life. She had an over-the-moon feeling about learning in the same school as what she felt like was her brilliant and terrifically bright older brother, Oscar. Caroline felt if he were ever to be tested, he would qualify as a genius. Caroline had a great admiration for her brother and all that he was capable of. In a way, she wanted to be just like him. They both craved adventure. The scraped knees from exploring the woods and climbing mountains and the pure dauntless minutes of excitement in the outdoors drew them both to appreciate nature. Caroline envied what she thought was Oscar's fun and spontaneous life. Being the only girl in the family, even among the cousins, and as you can imagine, Caroline felt she was shielded and sheltered from that "wild, adventurous" behavior Oscar enjoyed. Do not get me wrong. I would have loved to be like Caroline and be the only girl in the family. Even though the special treatment secluded Caroline, it made her feel special. Nevertheless, the family, in a peculiar way, put her on the pedestal of special treatment, again setting her apart and further contributing to her divergent feelings. Oscar was allowed to explore the world with endless possibilities, but Caroline was kept a little closer inside under the protective watch of her mother, grandmother, and aunts.

Caroline breathed a sigh of relief once she started school. Could it be true? Was she no longer under the watchful eyes of her granny, mother, and aunts? *Yes*, at least for a bit. She was excited about venturing out of her comfort zone and experiencing this little thing called life. Luckily, she had a best friend, Rachel Lane Foster, her next-door neighbor. Rachel attended the same school as Caroline and Oscar. They had high hopes of being placed in the same class. Unfortunately, due to their inseparable history of living next door to each other before kindergarten, their parents felt it would be best to keep them apart in school—different classes, completely separate. They believed this would keep us focused and out of "girl trouble" as they called it. At first, this was a difficult task for Caroline, but she was so excited and enthusiastic about starting school that she began to adapt and make friends quite naturally. Good thing, too! As it turns out, Caroline would not be in a class with Rachel until my tenth-grade year. She explained it as a short eighty-minute US history class. However, Caroline did admit that she and Rachel did get into a few shenanigans throughout their time together in school. As Caroline grew and made new friends apart from Rachel, she quickly realized how easy it was to connect with boys, rather than girls. I explained to Caroline that it was very easy for me as well. It was because it was just me and my brother growing up. Caroline seemed to agree because she seemed to have some expertise in being a professional GI Joe, *Stars Wars* expert, Army, and race cars background experience, thanks to her brother Oscar. Sidenote: do not let him fool you. He was a borderline Barbie doll / Ken doll fan as well. Caroline explained that on rare occasions, GI Joe, aka Oscar, would visit Barbie's dream house (her room) and play with her toys! I thought that was funny. I would say that occurred or was an infrequent occurrence in my household. I had to do boy stuff way more often than play with girl stuff.

FIGHTING DEMONS WHILE CHASING GOD!

Next thing Caroline knew, half of a school year had passed, and she was having a blast, learning, finding her creativity—in the block center, of course (which she never seemed to get enough time in; she loved building things), and the painting center (which she did not get enough time). Caroline is among the most creative and out-of-the-box thinkers I have ever met. Her curiosity and desire to discover and create were barely beginning to scratch the surface. She felt she had so much more to offer the world but wasn't allowed to.

Flash forward a few months, and it was time to celebrate what felt like her most significant birthday yet! She was turning six! The pure joy she felt with her current circumstances and overwhelming desire to learn was as wholesome as ever! Little did she know, in just twenty-eight days, on April 16, 1976, the curiosity, desire to learn, creativity, and overall enjoyment of life would be shattered by her first demon, a thief in the night who stole her innocence. The many conversations that Caroline and I have had over this have been too numerous to count. I explained to her that I had lost my father at a very young age. It has been so challenging to go through some of life's significant moments like learning how to drive, first boyfriend, first kiss, graduation, getting help to decide on what college to go to, having a dad walk you down the aisle, your very own daddy-daughter dance, and just simply missing that big hug of comfort of being in the arms of your daddy. Unlike Caroline, I don't remember much before the age of twelve. It is amazing how your brain and body physically protect you from trauma. Caroline suggested that it was the way God made us help protect us from the severe pain and trauma of remembering bad things or bad times that occur in our lives. During those conversations, I often told her how I wished I had had her strength and faith. She would quickly remind me that her power came from God. *"I can do all things through Christ that strengthens me" (Philippians 4:13).* Caroline reminded me often of how we only get the strength we need for that day; that is why we have to look to God constantly.

Yes, Caroline was six years old. Yes, she went to church every Sunday morning for worship. Yes, she knew who Jesus was. However, she explained how she was not at an age where she truly understood what it meant to have an actual relationship with Christ, a relationship where she could and would choose to depend on Him. She explained how that incident forced her, at such a young age, to learn what *true faith* looked and felt like. Looking back, I had to agree with Caroline and admit that if I, too, knew more about a steadfast relationship with God, I would have had the ability to see His promises and truths He prevails to show us through the Scripture. I now can see that Scripture was revealing its truth to me the entire time as it played out in my life. Caroline stated that her faith grew early on and strengthened more often than others. She explained that it was a constant battle of balance between being assertive and maintaining a true faith in God.

> *Humble yourselves, therefore, under the mighty hand of God so at the proper time he may exalt you, casting all of your anxieties on him, because he cares for you. (1 Peter 5:6–7 ESV)*

The first question that came to my mind as she shared her story was, How is a six-year-old supposed to humble herself so that God can exalt them? As Caroline explained, how unknowing she was at the time of her father's death, that God's planned days He had already written in His book for her were to be one day exalting her up so that she would share the Gospel with others like me. But to me, all I could imagine and my personal experience at a very young age was confusion and thoughts of what in the world was going on? Caroline continued to explain to me that it was at this stage in life that God was beginning the process of cultivating my heart, faith, trust, and mindset to know that there is and must be something more. Unfortunately, I couldn't see that. I often wonder if Caroline had been in my life at that time, she would have been able to guide me a little closer to God, or does that guidance need to come from God himself?

Further into scripture, Peter describes the attributes of Satan and what he is willing to do, and no, age does not matter if God has courageous plans to use you in His plan. Satan will stop at nothing.

FIGHTING DEMONS WHILE CHASING GOD!

> *Be sober minded; be watchful. Your adversary the Devil prowls around like a roaring lion, seeking someone to devour. (1 Peter 5:8)*

Notice that scripture is not telling you to be watchful as an adult or teenager. The devil wants to devour someone, and I'll tell you who he wants to devour: someone that God is wanting to use in His ministry. I'm sure you are thinking that doesn't include me, but it does. It includes everyone that has placed their faith, trust, and belief in Him for their salvation from hell. Continue delving deeper to look how you are included. First Peter 5: 9–10 says:

> Resist him, firm in your faith, knowing that the same kinds of suffering are being experienced by your brotherhood throughout the world. And after you have suffered a little while, the God of all grace, who has called you to his eternal glory in Christ.

Stopping at this point is as if saying that doesn't prove that Christ or God has called all of us who have faith in Him. That is where I ask you as the reader to continue delving into the word of truth and understanding the commands of God is crucial to the relationship of faith you claim to have.

Look at Matthew 18:18–20, which states:

> And Jesus came and said to them, "All authority in heaven and on earth has been given to me. Go therefore and make disciples of all nations, baptizing them in the name of the Father, and of the Son, and of the Holy Spirit, teaching them to observe all that I have commanded you. And behold, I am with you always, to the end of the age."

Wow! There it is, the command for everyone, including you. It is your calling and your instructions of what your purpose is here for. How, at six years old, did Caroline see that? Could have I noticed that? Why has it taken me so long to see that? How can we, as individuals who are facing trauma or grief, understand that it is just the preparation for God's calling on our lives? Some of you may even be saying the same thing in your teens, twenties, thirties, or even forties, but not at such a young age. I had no idea. When sharing my experience with Carline, I explained that all I knew was that my life had gone from the ordinary traditional American family of mother, father, and two kids to a nightmare within a few seconds. During one of my conversations with Caroline, she helped me understand the excellent thing to learn, which is that I am not the only one that God started preparing young. Scripture gives us several individuals who have had their lives disrupted or turned upside down due to the persecution of evil, demons, and Satan.

Just a few examples. Isaac had to trust his father, Abraham, knew what he was doing when he was being tied down as a sacrifice. Moses's mother was having to be put him in the Nile River for fear of him being killed by the Pharaoh. He then grew up in a home of the people that were oppressing his birth family and people, only later to have a desire to reconnect with his heritage, that when he tries to reach out to members of his own people, they reject him for his anger and rage that he had taken out on the Egyptian, excusing him of the same violence toward them. King David was just a shepherd watching over sheep when God called him to face a giant. Joseph and Mary had to flee to Egypt from Bethlehem due to a kill order given on all the children to stop the rise of Christ.

The relationship that Christians have with God is so much deeper and richer than we as humans could ever fathom, yet God still desires that relationship. God still desires to use us in capacities that we are not even aware of. Preparation is the key. So during this tragic event, all that can be said is, but God, since I had not developed a relationship with God at this time.

CHAPTER 2

Death as a Demon

The thief only comes to steal and kill and destroy. I came that they may have life and have it abundantly.

—John 10:10

April 16, 1976, the kindergarten classes were learning to square dance. Caroline's class and her best friend Rachel's class had gone to the main building to be a part of the learning and celebrations in the kindergarten and first-grade combination class. Caroline's partner, of course, ended up being one of her first crushes but ultimately her very best guy friend throughout all of her elementary and secondary school years, Charlie Heston. They always seemed to be partnered together mostly likely because they were about the same height and his name came after hers alphabetically. She told me that they always lined up the boys/girls in her class to prevent them from misbehaving. I find that amusing as today in education that hardly ever works because the boys tend to tease the girls. As Caroline began to describe the details of her memory of that day, it made me wonder if I would ever remember the details of my loss. Anyway, she explained all of the students sitting on each side of the room with all the desks and chairs moved to the back so that they would have a long path to have a couple of different groups able to stand and participate in the activity. She continued to explain how this was some sort of cultural concept that her grade level had been learning. She described a fun unit of learning about Johnny Appleseed and how springtime was the best time of year to plant trees.

She said that they had gotten to make caramel apples and ate them a few days before. She reassured me that she could tell there was just something very different about this day. She said for the first time in a long time, she was reticent and felt a distance or an unusual feeling as if something terrible was wrong. She and Charlie had just finished their first or second turn at the square-dancing concept. Then all of a sudden, she seemed to have a burst of happiness. Then all at once, she remembered looking at the clock, feeling as if something had just occurred or time had stopped. She said that she remembered drawing into herself very quickly with her emotions and tracing the checked lines on the pale blue teacher's desk. It was as if she had no awareness of time and was unsure how much time passed. It didn't seem too long after that uncomfortable feeling that the office called over the loudspeaker to her individual class that Caroline was needed in the office for dismissal. She felt a minor panic in her stomach because she couldn't recall a reason for going home, and she wondered if there was something to that uncomfortable feeling, had something terrible happened. She wasn't sick but was starting to feel that way. The teacher helped her gather her belongings together, and she went to the door to stand and wait. Someone was coming to the classroom to get her.

As she slowly walked out into the hallway, she saw Martha, the lady who worked in the Copper Mill office with her mother. She thought this was bizarre because Martha was considered an old maid who had never been married or had children. Confused, they walked silently, thinking, *Why must Martha come to her school?* She didn't know what to say to her, and Martha didn't know what to say to Caroline, so they walked silently to the office's second floor. When they got to the main office, as Caroline was about to walk through the door, she could see her uncle, a deputy sheriff, who worked at the Lumberyard, the assistant principal standing outside his office, and her Sunday school teacher. Caroline explained how she thought it was peculiar and began to tense up inside. These individuals were people who were not limited and amounted to much interaction. She had spent the majority of her time next door at Rachel's house, with her granny and her aunts growing up, so her nervousness became fear. Why were they there? What was going on?

They walked Caroline into the assistant principal's office. Her mother and Oscar were already there. Her brother, who was twelve at the time, looked to have his stern face on and was like, "What is going on?" almost in an angry voice. Her mother, very lovingly and patiently, tried to console him as Caroline came in, and the door shut behind me. Her mother was trying to be strong but was crying and had been crying and just blurted out, "Children, your father is dead."

It all seemed to be happening so very fast that it went directly over Caroline's comprehension level, and she was confused. She very meekly asked her mother, "What do you mean?"

Oscar began to burst out crying straight away and then shouted, "He is dead! Caroline, dead, as in never coming back!" Her mother continued to console her brother and tried to get him to calm down, and it was at the moment Caroline met her first encounter with the demon of death. I explained to Caroline that I had never seen death as a demon. She began to explain that he had taken it all—her memories of her father, the image of her father, the remainder of that day, and every day after that until she was almost a teenager. She had to begin therapy to help her mind and body remember what her father was like. Even still, the memories she said were foggy. Caroline explained to me that during the seventies, therapy and seeing a psychiatrist was not encouraged. But fortunately, her family began to see her pain and felt that the only way to help her was through a professional. I told Caroline that when I had my first encounter with death, I felt numb and that I was supposed to be strong because everyone around me was falling to pieces. I also explained to Caroline that our family hardly ever discusses their feelings—whether they are happy, mad, sad, or disappointed—or we just don't discuss stuff like that. That is why sometimes I seem very skeptical about people who just want to discuss all these emotions and society talking so much about emotional health. Don't get me wrong, my visit with Caroline has begun to be my therapy, and it has helped to uncover so many buried emotions that have, over time, taken a physical toll on my body. It was amazing when I was explaining to Caroline that for over twenty-five years, my body has been functioning in a fight-or-flight response and that my adrenal glands had stopped working. In one of my most recent visits with Caroline, she said that when she was younger, she began acting out, doing things on purpose to get attention, and simply getting into trouble, which was highly unlike her, that her family saw these as signs that she needed help and knew that if they didn't step in soon, then she would begin to unravel. Her family found a Christian therapist who helped her see God's plan for her life. They helped bring her to an understanding of God's word and promises, which she has begun to guide and help me. I must admit not all my memories were stolen entirely from my childhood.

I remember being taught coping mechanisms during good times when it was just my tiny family of three. Still, unfortunately, I remember many bad times for my family of three. Caroline explained that Satan comes into an individual's life at the point of weakness to destroy any joy, hope, or seeds that had been planted to serve the Lord at Sunday church services. Now at such a young age, I didn't understand that. All I can honestly remember is floundering the next few years, searching for my father, hoping that maybe it wasn't real. I know, for a long time, every time I would see a truck like my father would drive, I would search and search to see if he might be him driving so we could chase him down to ask why he left us. I found out later in life that my brother had also done that. Caroline explained that it was my humanity trying to comprehend God's plan. She said that at this point, I had not been given enough information or shown scripture that would allow God's voice to come through to help ease my and my brother's pain. Caroline continued her story to help me and my healing process. It was amazing that this was the first time I could relate to someone who had experienced something very similar to what I had experienced. She explained how this healing process would use family, friendships, church family, and even strangers. She asked if I recalled her friendship with her best friend and next-door neighbor, Rachel, which was the first of many relationships to

FIGHTING DEMONS WHILE CHASING GOD!

become much more substantial. She explained how she practically lived at her house for the next little while. It seemed easier to not think about her father, not see the sadness in her mother's eyes, and to stop arguing with Oscar because he was simply angry all the time. She explained that, especially during the summer months, she would stay at her house for weeks at a time, and finally, she would have to go home, but to what? Loneliness? Even though she was in her house with her family, she said it didn't often feel like a family or home. It was as if everyone would retreat to designated areas and only communicate at dinner or when watching TV. There have been times in my life that I felt as though I could relate to being in a house full of people yet feeling completely alone. Caroline told me to be careful that I was the preying enemy of Satan and his evil spirits preying on the weak by putting thoughts and feelings into our minds and hearts that were untrue or crippling to ask for help. I often wondered what type of thoughts from Satan and his evil spirits were being placed into my head, my heart, my mom's head and heart, and my brother's head and heart. I must say one thing that I can take away most from my visits with Caroline is her explanation that we are never alone, God is always with us, and it is our choice if we decide to listen to Satan and his evil spirits or if we chose to seek God first and foremost. Listening to Caroline's story about her life and growing up would help me remember memories I thought I had lost again, some good and some bad. I have often asked Caroline why this is, and she said that I became the person I am because of what I experienced and my choices in handling those situations. She explained that often our memories are not entirely accurate and that our minds are trying to protect our mental and emotional well-being. Our body only allows us to remember when it feels that we are ready to experience the greatest joy or the horrific trauma. I think it is not our brains that will enable us to remember but God who allows us to remember. Scripture tells us that he will not put on us more than we can handle. I think God knows the right time and moment of healing when we should remember events or circumstances to bring healing, comfort, and closure. One of the many stories I could relate to Caroline was her coping mechanisms of pain and trauma experience.

Caroline began to explain that she started acting out, telling everyone close to her that she hated them and wanted to live somewhere other than her house. She would repeatedly argue with Oscar and her mother, and at the end of every argument, she would explain that she hated them. She explained that she would do these things because she constantly felt excluded from her newly established family of three. She explained how she was never old enough for conversations that Oscar and her mother had. She said she understood because he was so much older than she was. However, there would be times when Oscar would be sitting in the kitchen, listening to her day while she entertained herself. That is when she told me that her imagination began to trickle back, and she found a new love of reading that started to bloom. She explained that she and her family's church attendance became more sporadic, but that was when she began to dig into God's Word independently. Sometimes, her family would go all out for church, be at every service that opened doors and participate in all the different activities the church had to offer. However, there were times when her family would simply stop going.

Caroline said that her church attendance became a guessing game of whether her mom needed Jesus that week. I began to ask Caroline how this played into her relationship with Christ, her family, and healing. She began to tell me that this all played into the hand of Satan very well. The seed that God had planted in her was not getting watered or nurtured. It was starving. I was starving. Caroline was dying for answers, attention, being noticed in her own home, and trying to impress her mother with her grades, yet at the same time acting out in rage when she was ignored. Yes, gaining her mother's approval started very early. It seemed to Caroline that if she were academically brilliant, she would finally get praise or "way to go" from her mother. However, it also seemed to be short-lived because once she achieved a goal once, she would have to do better the next time to get a higher achievement or award; otherwise, it was expected of her.

It was during this time the dynamics of the family changed. Everyone was so worried about Oscar and not so much about Caroline. It's funny how society and social theory decide when a father is absent, the primary concern should be the boy instead of the girl because a boy needs his father. However, society and social theory rarely examine the importance of father-daughter relationships. There are tons of memes and information out there about grown women being emotionally unstable because they have so-called daddy issues. Yet research has not gone into helping fatherless young girls handle the life stressors that occur to young girls without fathers. Caroline felt that she was taken off the pedestal she had been placed on by her family and father and was replaced with Oscar by her mother's concern for her son to grow up without a father. He had become the golden child, and Caroline more of what society would call the black sheep. It seemed that Caroline never felt that she was good enough for praise, encouragement, and support or cherished sufficient to be fully included in her family of three. Caroline didn't want me to think that she had been just tossed to the wayside. She explained that she did receive praise and encouragement, but it was given in a much different manner and less often than Oscar who received a wealth of encouragement and praise. Actions often speak louder than words. Since the 1970s, research has been done on the five different love languages. The essence of grand displays of encouragement and praise for Oscar was not how Caroline received it. She received it in a more subtle or obscure method, which made it difficult for her to understand that it was indeed praise, support, and encouragement. Even though the various methods of praise and encouragement were not meant to be intentional by Caroline and Oscar's mother, it became a painful process for Caroline. She felt as though she was in constant competition with her brother and sometimes even competing with her own mother. Caroline saw this difference in behavior as the primary focus seemed to fall on her brother because he was a male. At this point, the feeling of being a bit different or set apart from the rest of her family became more prominent, even noticeable to others.

Some of the deeper conversations that Caroline and I have had address the elephant in the room, so to speak. What type of emotional impact was this having on her and her knowledge of who God was? It is funny that she will always smile really big and laugh and explain that she would seek comfort, praise, and encouragement from the Lord. I often asked, "How did you do that?" She would admit to having her own little praise and worship sessions when she was at home alone.

She explained that there was one specific time she and her bus driver had been talking about Jesus, true friends, and how bad the world was getting. She left the bus that day so fired up for Christ that she had shouted, telling Satan that she and the other Christians of the world were going to take him down. She stated that she was waving her hands and stomping on the floor as if stomping on Satan himself. Caroline admitted that when she needed praise, encouragement, or just to feel hope, she would have her own praise session and take her anger and frustration out by positively shouting unto the Lord and stomping the devil always helped too. I said that sounded so fulfilling and that I had similar experiences except when I was moved by the spirit that much I would have crying blurring tears, then begin to sing and shout the praises of the Lord. It was as if Caroline was telling me that all the encouragement, praise, or support I needed, I had already in God; I just needed to learn to seek him out to receive it. Every time I think of those times, I quickly remember one of my favorite verses.

> Then you will call upon Me and come and pray to Me, and I will listen to you. You will seek Me and find Me when you search for Me with all your heart. (Jeremiah 29:12–13 ESV)

My time spent with Caroline has been helping me understand how to truly seek God, not just seek but to actually chase God. The demon of rejection played a role in Caroline's self-perception and self-worth—the constant rejections from conversations that were being had between her mother and brother. She told me often that she was never old enough or asked to leave because it was something I didn't need to know. The pushing away seemed to begin with her mother, not only from her but it also felt at times she didn't want Caroline to Oscar either. Satan began to use this demon to really torment Caroline because she became self-conscious if other family members, teachers, friends, or even pets would reject her.

It didn't help that Oscar was so much older than her because he would often reject her presence because she was the baby sister and it was cool to have her hanging around. Even though this was a normal teenage brother reaction, it was nevertheless painful to Caroline because she was still seeing it as rejection. She had gone from feeling like a princess to being the baby that gets thrown out with the bath water. These very feelings of rejection became a very long-running mind game from other demons, which were trying to instill doubt, fear, anxiety, and lies so that she would lose confidence in who God had in mind for her to become. It is amazing how quickly our value and worth decline when we allow Satan and his demons to have a field day within our thoughts.

The death of Caroline's father began to eat away at not only Caroline, Oscar, and her mom but it was beginning to eat away at her dear granny, aunts, and uncles. Conflict arose between her mother and her father's family. Caroline being so young and trying to comprehend loss, Oscar was angry at the world, and her mother was in unimaginable pain and trying to keep it together while also raising two kids on her own. Each in their own time, moments began to lash out at everyone. Grief is something that—in its various stages, I think—can be considered a demon of sorts too. I know that it felt like it at times when I have had to deal with deaths in my life. There are times when you are extremely sad from despair and angry with anything that is good because you don't feel like you deserve it, and finally comes the feeling of hopelessness, and you are constantly waiting for that other shoe to drop. Caroline explained to me that when someone experiences a tremendous loss, dealing with that pain takes a toll on the body and mind emotionally, spiritually, and physically. The death of my own father I know took a drastic toll on my own family of three, as well as my extended family. My own granny was tremendously hurt as well. She had lost her son that was her go-to for everything, especially since she had also lost my grandfather, to a firearm accident, just a few years prior. It was as if my father had become the support system that she needed after my grandpa's death. When a loved one dies, it makes you well aware of how much a family needs to forgive others but, most of all, forgive themselves because, in times of grief, we are never our true selves. Caroline explained to me that often the forgiveness that we should give others and ourselves during the grieving process that doesn't get forgiven turns into bitterness and resentment, and individuals begin to put up their defenses toward everyone. She said that it is when those defenses go up that the person grieving tends to hurt those closest to them. She told me that was what happened to her family; different members would react or act out due to their pain and hurt other members of her family. When it was time for accountability, everyone was so hurt that no one wanted to take accountability unless everyone took accountability. I find that amusing now because I watch clips on TikTok with phrases that say things like, "People get mad at your disrespectful reaction but never want to discuss their inappropriate behavior that made you have a disrespectful reaction in the first place." I find that to be more true in society today than ever in my lifetime. Caroline deals with instances like that all the time, she says. She says that is when prayer and seeking God to change the hearts of others is really all you can do because it doesn't matter how much we want someone to change, God is the only one who can change a heart.

Caroline has often explained to me that she has been in meetings with families, and they are so hurt, and in different stages of grief, they begin lashing out, "It's your fault he is dead," "If you hadn't wanted so much," "You can't stand that he loved me more than he loved you," "You'll never see these children again," etc. In reality, it was the response to such a deep and desperate hurt that they both took out on each other. Lots of hurt, anger, and bitterness between family members can generate sometimes lifelong fractures that never heal. Pain and loss are weak areas that the enemy will exploit to cause the most harm in people, families, and individuals. Unfortunately, the demon of pain had succeeded in all areas of people's lives. Satan knows how to destroy the essence of family, and that is his goal because it contradicts what God intended—a loving family. As I look back, over some of the devastating circumstances of my life, other demon culprits that come to mind in destroying a family, friendship, and work environment have been pride. And if we recall, pride was the original sin of Satan himself. Satan wanted to be just like God, and his pride in his skill, talent, and self is the very reason he fell from glory in the first place. Pride will destroy a family, and it will also destroy a person.

Shortly after Caroline's father died, she and Oscar only stayed off and on with her granny. The difference of pain is either demonizing or silence. Caroline never recalled her granny ever speaking negatively about her mother in front of her, but she always assumed that her granny did not like her mother. Although, Caroline's mother didn't hold back the negativity about her father's family, especially when they would get into an argument. Caroline has often explained that it was almost like her mother was doing her best to convince her and Oscar to take her side and discard her father's family. In reflection, looking back, Caroline understood that was done only out of hurt and fear of one day being alone. During traumatic times, lives are forever altered.

Caroline is just glad that she received the therapy and emotional support that she needed, which helped prepare her to be able to help individuals like me. Oftentimes, I wish that there would have been interventions of family counseling and therapy for my mother, myself, and my brother to be able to express our pain and anguish in a more healthy manner instead of taking it out on each other. The fractures that it has created have been so costly. I so desperately want to explain that I understand the emotional trauma that was caused by the loss of my dad was not done deliberately, yet it was still caused.

I could tell that hurt and anger was overtaking my mother. As I remember the tough times, I realize how much God was in control and how it was those times he was developing my faith, strength, and dependency on him instead of my earthly family. Oftentimes, I would ask my mom about my father. I don't recall her ever really saying anything encouraging about him other than he worked all the time. I can only imagine her desire to not talk about my father because it caused her too much pain. Sometimes, I believe that it caused me pain as well, not knowing him or his family like I would have desired to increase my feelings of being lost because the thing was, I was unable to truly remember my dad. Many times when would walk in on conversations between my mother and brother, discussing my dad, my mom would always ask me to leave the room because I was "too young" to understand.

It is amazing, as mothers, what we do to protect our kids from pain. As a mother myself, I find myself holding information back because I do not want to ruin or muddy their perception of various circumstances. However, as a child just looking for answers, that type of protection built up resentment, anger, and hostility toward my protectors. During one of my many conversations with Caroline, I shared a conversation with her that I have never really understood the purpose or point of the conversation about my dad with my mother. It is one conversation that was had many times and has had a lasting impact of hurt and pain. I remember asking my mom if my dad really loved me, and she told me that when I was born, the snow was falling, and the doctors and nurses were watching people slide around in the hospital parking lot while she was in active labor. My father had gone down to the cafeteria to get something to eat. When he got back up and realized I was born and that I was a girl, he walked right back out upset because he wanted a boy. I was told that he was not excited about having a girl. This story was told to me over and over again. For someone wanting answers and a simple connection to her father, the story crushed me to think that my father didn't want me.

I went the majority of my childhood and young adulthood thinking that I had been rejected by one of the people that had made me from the very beginning. However, Mom would always add on to the story, but that was okay because she was elated that I was a little girl and that it was going to be me and her, and if no one else loved her, she knew that I always would. Sometimes, I wonder if she told me this story so that I would not miss my father as much. Caroline tried to ease my pain by explaining that maybe it was a simple story to show how badly my mother wanted me. One factor that I didn't consider was the main individual that loved me and wanted me, and that was God. Oftentimes we allow the enemy to use our pain, suffering, and insecurities to take advantage of so that he can move individuals further away from God's purpose. The enemy will use others to manipulate to maintain a sense of loyalty and love. Unfortunately, this became the foundation of my relationship with my mother. Over time, the problem and uneasy feelings that I was having were as if something was still off with me.

Years later, I would learn from my granny and aunts that this story couldn't be further from the truth. My dad was over the moon that I was a girl and that I looked just like him. He would take me everywhere with him, and I was truly a daddy's girl when I was little. Unfortunately, these are precious memories that I was robbed of when death came to my family and took my father.

> The Lord is my Shepherd; I shall not want. He makes me lie down in green pastures. He leads me through still waters. He restores my soul. He leads me in the paths of righteousness for his name's sake. Even though I walk through the valley of shadow of death, I will fear no evil, for you are with me, for thy rod and staff they comfort me. (Psalm 23:1–4 ESV).

During my healing process Caroline helped me to see that it is as if this verse was summing up my life up to this point. I wanted beg her how was I supposed to see this as a child of six, walking through the valley of the shadow of death, fearing evil, seems to be all I can concentrate on. Today, looking at that point of my life, I can see that I was on Christ's shoulders in that valley. He hid me from evil things that were going on around me. He protected me from conversations that I never needed to hear. He protected me from situations that could have destroyed me for life. He shielded every advance of the enemy, to keep me and the seed that He had begun to cultivate on the path of righteousness. It is funny that when we are in the storm, all we see is the storm. But when we look back, all we can see is God. Why are we as mankind so quick to turn on Him when He is so quick to pick us up? As I imagine, the cosmic spiritual battle raging around us right now, God is shielding us, stabbing the enemy, crushing demons, pushing us in a protected area so that He can defeat the enemy. Satan gets His boosts of energy by devouring the very ones God plans to use in spectacular ways. The problem is we know that we are called, we have a mission, but we tend to forget who we are, when we are where we are.

Sometimes, those valleys are just overpowering to our human capacity. That is why depending on our own strength, our own wisdom, and our own power will not allow God's capacity to be revealed to us as it was not revealed to me at the age of six, but God!

CHAPTER 3

Flickering Hope Quickly Squashed

> For God so loved the world that he gave his only Son, that whosoever believes in Him should not perish but have eternal life. For God did not send his Son into the world to condemn the world, but in order that the world might be saved through him. Whoever believes in him is not condemned, but whoever does not believe is condemned already, because he has not believed in the name of the only Son of God.
>
> —John 3:16–18

It was Caroline who inspired me to write my thoughts down. Healing past trauma can be difficult because coping mechanisms tend to bury the toughest of pain and trauma. She explained that as he worked through her own trauma and grief due to the thief stealing her memories prior to her father's passing, she often struggled with the fact of not remembering the treasured time she had with him and her family during those years. Caroline admitted she could recall that her mother drew close to her mom (Caroline's grandma) but, unfortunately, she explained how those memories were impacted as well. It was only three short years later that the demon of death would again come knocking on Caroline's door, finishing what he had started, the destruction of her family and her desire to learn about God. However, she could remember some of her time was spent on and off again at church. One of those memories is of a very special night service that she was attending. Yes, being in the Bible Belt, hell, fire, and brimstone were often the topics of the sermons. That night, she spoke of what a wonderful service it was, but it was a hell, fire, and brimstone service by her beloved pastor, Blake Lee. She went into detail of the overwhelming feeling that she had within side her. Normally, after the service would finish, the kids would go outside to play tag while waiting on the parents to finish socializing. Playing tag was not on Caroline's radar.

She had just heard a message that declared what her eternity was going to be like. It was eternal damnation in the lake of fire with Satan and all of his demons. She explained how not knowing God as her savior was going to put her suffering even more than she had ever suffered. She came to the realization that she was going to burn alive forever. She wouldn't see her family's loved ones, she wouldn't see her daddy ever again. It was as if that message was the very message that seed planted a few years back needed to burst forth and start to sprout.

After service, Caroline went straight to the car and waited for her brother, Oscar, and mother. She explained being quiet the whole ride home, which wasn't unusual. She felt as if she never fit into the conversations of her brother and mother. The connection or relationship just wasn't there. She told me she always felt like an outsider. It was funny as she explained always felt like an outsider to me; I listened, relating so intensely to also feeling like an outsider in my own family. Unfortunately, I still do, but I think there is a purpose for that. After arriving home, Caroline's mother could tell something was bothering Caroline but didn't push the issue. Caroline jumped out of the car, went to her room, and sat on the floor, staring at her reflection for a while. She was supposed to be packing a suitcase because her brother had a baseball tournament in Patrick County, Virginia. They were going to stay in Preacher Blake's mountain house that he had built for his family to vacation in. His wife, Beverly, was going up to visit her son and daughter-in-law and was going to stay there as well.

Caroline finally had sat on her floor with such dread and fear of going to hell with an eternity of fire that she couldn't take it anymore. She rushed to her mother's room and climbed up on her bed where she was reading her Bible. Caroline fumbled for words, then finally asked her mother how she could not go to hell. Caroline's mother was surprised but gently began to ask if that was what was bothering her. Caroline told her yes, so much that her stomach was starting to hurt. Her mother hugged me real big and then began to water that seed. She showed Caroline various scriptures such as *John 3:16, which says, "For God so loved the world that he gave his only Son, that whoever believes in him will not perish but have eternal life,"* which is the foundation and why God would do something for mankind. She talked to her about how Adam and Eve were deceived by Satan in the garden, and that was what separated us in fellowship with God. She then took me to *Romans 6:23, which states, "That the wages of sin is death, but the free gift of God is eternal life in Christ Jesus."* Then to *Romans 3:23, which says, "For all have sinned and come short of the glory of God."* From there she took me over to *Romans 10:8–10*, and it states:

> But what does it say? "The word is near you, in your mouth and in your heart" (that is the word of faith that we proclaim); because, if you confess with your mouth that Jesus is Lord and believe in your heart that God raised him from the dead, you will be saved. For with the heart one believes and is justified, and with the mouth one confesses and is saved."

It seemed so easy and simple. Yet again, at the age of eight, Caroline was confused. How could this be so easy? Then her mother explained faith. She sighted scripture from Ephesians. Caroline realized it was at this point that she understood true salvation, the solidity of a relationship with her heavenly Father, and why the book of Ephesians quickly became her favorite book of the Bible. I myself also had a similar encounter getting to know God. But it was a struggle for me because of the inconsistency I had with getting to know the Lord. I asked Caroline if she ever felt that sometimes she felt on fire for God and then other times she felt ice-cold. She admitted that she had felt that way, and she had also felt lukewarm for God as well. We all know how God feels about being lukewarm. Just as John writes a letter to the church of Laodicea.

> *So because you are lukewarm, and neither hot nor cold, I will spit you out of My mouth. (Revelation 3:16)*

> *For by grace you have been saved through faith. And this is not your own doing; it is the gift of God, not a result of works, so that no one may boast. For we are his workmanship, created in Christ Jesus for good works, which God prepared beforehand, that we should walk in them. (Ephesians 2:8–10 ESV)*

Realizing that there are others in the world who have had struggles similar to mine and their relationship with God has had its struggles of connection, I began to understand grace and that although we go through trials and tribulations, we are granted grace and redemption for the fallible choices that we decide to make as humans. Lord knows that I have made fallible choices, but it has been the grace that he has granted me that has gotten me to where I am. My own salvation decision was a warm summer night in mid-July of 1988, it was then that I truly accepted Christ as my Savior and began to form that relationship and connection. It was amazing that I had found a friend that I could share my experience with and how I had never felt a sense of peace like I felt that night prior. Caroline began to explain the amount of joy, peace, and reassurance that salvation provides. We would spend eternity in heaven with Christ, the Man that suffered and died for my sins—past, present, and future. We would get to meet the Creator of our universe, mankind, the very one that gave so much thought and preparation to our existence. We would be able to ask the questions of curiosity that often plague all of us. She reassured me that we both would also hopefully get to see our fathers again.

FIGHTING DEMONS WHILE CHASING GOD!

This portion of Caroline's timeline, however vague, church was finally becoming a big part of her family's lives. She explained as if they were finally beginning to get up and make efforts to get to church for more services, besides morning worship service. She and Oscar were getting to do things that pertained to kids and Christ. It brought back her excitement to learn and find out all the amazing miracles that God performed for the Israelites. Often, in the evenings, she would read my little New Testament that she had received from the Gideons passing them out on the school campus. Her favorite story to read was of how Christ was born, along with the Psalms. Her mother would often tell her and Oscar to go to bed, and she would turn her light out, but once the house got quiet, she would turn back on her lamplight and just read and read until she fell asleep. Reading was a common soothing experience that we had in common. We would reminisce over the joy and excitement that we got out of reading the Gospel.

During the late eighties and early nineties, in the South, there were lots of tent revivals, especially in the fall and spring. Almost every year, Pastor William Hanks would come to Stokes Dale High School and sell out the stadium for the message of God to be brought to the community. During those days, discussion of your faith, religion, and even worshiping the Lord was expected in the Bible Belt. It saddens my heart to know that sin has brought us to the point that we are now having mass shootings at school and community functions, when thirty years ago, we were having revivals and praise and worship concerts. Evil and sin can make everyone fall, even the most upright Christian. I know myself that I have fallen short of living the life God would be proud of. I just want to one day stand before him and he'd say, "Well done, good and faithful servant." The sad thing is that there have been so many times each of us has not been that faithful servant while God is always faithful.

As I reflect and discuss my battles with demons sent to distract or block my path for the Lord with Caroline, I have recognized that I thought I had only faced two, but there have been several since my father passed away. Those demons came in many forms—some seemed to be friends, family, and even spiritual leaders, and others were blatant and obvious. I was finally coming to grips and understanding that I would not see my father again in this life. Caroline explained that accepting that can be a battle in itself, and since I had lost my father at such a young age, she understood the questions, fears, loneliness, and feelings of being lost all too well because she had experienced them. I explained to Caroline that even though I was starting to move forward, it didn't deter me from looking at every white Chevy truck to see if it just might be my dad. She helped me understand that there would always be a part of me that looked for him on special occasions and events. I must admit she was right; even to this day, I long to talk to him, share my frustration of not having him in my life, or get to do some of the special father-daughter things most other daughters get to do with their fathers.

One cold winter Sunday morning, Caroline's family was in church, and it was almost the very end of the service. For some reason, as Pastor Blake was wrapping up the service, the phone began to ring. Remembering this was in the late eighties, so no cell phones. This was the landline phone of the church. It was very strange and weird. It rang and rang then stopped.

A few minutes later, it began to ring and ring again. Finally, someone must have answered it. To Coraline, an eight-year-old, it was a huge distraction. The congregation stood up to sing the closing hymnal, and someone came to get her mother. She told Caroline and her brother, Oscar, to stay there, and she would be right back. Once the church was about to be dismissed, a few members of the church came and got Oscar and Caroline during the final prayer. They walked them slowly to the nursery where the phone had been answered. That is when the demon of death made himself known to her family once again. She stood looking around at everyone staring. She said she suddenly knew what it felt like as an animal at the zoo and being stared at. Her mother took their hands and explained that their Mimi, who was her mother, had died. The shock of the situation held Caroline back as she thought, *Really, again, what is going on?* She didn't understand what was happening. Why is this happening to her family? Why all the tragedy? All of these questions were rolling through my mind, all the while people just staring at their helpless or what she felt like was a weakened family.

Caroline wanted to go with her mother to get some answers and clarity, but her mother felt that it was best if she and Oscar stayed with friends from church. The whole time Caroline talked about her Mimi with her friend and all the emotions and questions going unanswered, but she explained how her biggest frustration was that her mother had shut her out again, pushed her away, excluded her from being a part of a huge life-altering situation and handed her off to others to deal with her and her brother. Caroline explained that she felt her mother and brother were all they had was each other as a support system, and it was like their love, strength, and support was not good enough or what her mother wanted. I explained to Caroline that there have been many times that I have felt as if I had been tossed to the side. It was always as if I never quite fit in with the crowd or even the family for that matter, but the difference between Caroline and me was she was given the support to help her understand, and I am getting that same help just several years down the road.

Now, of course, looking back, Caroline explained that she feels her mother probably did what any mother would have done to protect her children from any further pain than necessary. She explained that her mother was trying to bear all the pain herself and that in some of the circumstances that I have shared with her, that is probably the same concept my mother was following. However, what most people don't understand is that even though we feel like we are protecting someone unless we give that person a voice to explain what they need protecting from, it can later add to the trauma that person is experiencing, instead of preventing it. Oftentimes, we should try to look at things from all perspectives and be open-minded that in a time like that, she was experiencing death, rejection, and trauma from the child's point of view. Caroline found it difficult to relate to how an adult would have handled it because at first, it was not discussed. I do know that looking at my own suffering and trauma, exclusion is not the answer. Caroline explained that exclusion is not the answer, but full immersion is not the answer as well.

Within the last three years, Caroline had lost her husband and mother; the two people that were the closest to her besides Oscar and Caroline. Her mental capacity went into survival mode very quickly. At this point, she was just trying to make it through the day. The death of her Mimi created an even bigger gaping hole in her mother. Caroline's mother began to fill it with all sorts of things that would make her feel less empty. When we have an emptiness or a hole in us, we tend to turn to whatever will fix it. I know that I have turned in many different directions, looking to fill the gaping hole in me. However, we forget to look at the only one who can feel that hole and that is God.

Caroline's mother started dating six months after her father died and had already one, if not two, failed relationships. Her mother hated being alone. Mimi was the glue keeping Caroline's mother held together. It seems that at this point, Caroline's mother had made it her mission to find Oscar and Caroline a father and her a husband, since it was rarely unheard of in the Bible Belt to have a single widowed mother around. It was the belief of the South and a lot of the country that a woman needed a man to survive, but a man did not need a woman.

After a few failed relationships, Caroline felt like her mom was determined to be a groundbreaker of that theory because if she was not engrossed in her work, she was signing up for night classes to get her bachelor's degree. Caroline seems to think that her mother was trying everything from church, work, school, men, really anything to fill the void that she was feeling. The problem is that she did not realize because she was so focused on filling that void her mother was creating a void in Caroline and Oscar's lives. Now granted because boys sports were played later in the day, Caroline's mother was in attendance for the majority of Oscar's events and rarely ever at Caroline's. There was a difference in childhood memories that impacted one child more than the other. This was the same scenario in my own childhood. In one of my many venting sessions with Caroline, I told her that I always got excuses of "Well, I can't get off work early enough," "I can't miss class," or "I had some stuff I needed to finish up." Don't get me wrong. Just one excuse after another, and it is frustrating. Why couldn't a mother see the pain that these excuses have put on her children? I didn't realize how painful excuses could be until I missed my own daughter's volleyball awards night because I was getting my nails done and celebrating upon getting into Perdue University. It was her explaining this to me that it really hit home though the excuses may be important to you or valid, to a child who is expecting full support from a parent there is no excuse valid to miss a function. My drive and work ethic comes from my mother, mainly because that is what I witnessed on a daily routine.

Often, in our lives, we feel the burn or the sting of rejection. It is hard to overcome or to seek out answers as to why we are being rejected, especially for a child. In this situation, I was not being rejected due to malice or hardness toward me. I was rejected out of survival. The rejection from the perspective of a mother was not seen that way but seen as a method of protection, instead of rejection. However, this is where understanding the damage done by evil, a demon, or Satan himself. We as Christians have to be open to the fact areas where we saw protection, others perceive it as rejection. Once an individual is put into that survival mode, bringing clarity to an area of weakness is often difficult to do, so therefore the trauma incurs.

There were many times in my life that sometimes we were all running the same rat race of survival of the fittest. Many times, I wonder why I would even be in that type of race. It goes back to scripture. We are all called by God in some form to contribute to His ministry and His kingdom, whether it be financially, personal time, education, oneself as a mission, prayerfully, through song, or preaching the Gospel—we all have been given special talents that demonstrate we are called for a purpose.

> *As you come to him, a living stone rejected by men but in the sight of God chosen and precious, you yourselves like having living stones built up like a house, to be a holy priesthood, to offer spiritual sacrifices acceptable to God through Jesus Christ. (1 Peter 2:4–5 ESV)*

Granted as I read this scripture now, its meaning and substance that it resonates with me brings the clarity I could have used when I was young. However, if I had clarity at a young age, would that have altered the trials and circumstances that I needed to face to mold me into the woman that I am today, accepting the challenge of being an obedient follower of Christ? It is amazing at how the Holy Spirit reveals scripture and comforting words to you when you are at just the right maturity level that God sees fit in providing the clarity that has been long needed. I love the concept that God's timing is not always our timing, but it is His timing that is so much more perfect for us. I am reminded of the story of Lazarus, Mary, and Martha. According to the Gospel of John, Lazarus, Mary, and Martha were dear friends of Jesus during his ministry on earth. Jesus was in the next town over when He received word that Lazarus was very ill, and his sisters were requesting that Jesus come at once to heal their brother. Christ, however, was not worried because he stated that this illness would not lead to death but would only glorify God through Christ Jesus, and delayed four days in going to see Lazarus.

When Christ finally arrived, Mary and Martha came rushing to Him, distraught that He had delayed coming, and now their brother had died. Christ tried to comfort them and told them that their brother would rise again, but they were confused and didn't understand because he had been dead four days. Christ explained that He was the life and resurrection, and whoever believes in Him will have eternal life. The women and crowd still did not understand, so Christ called Lazarus out of the grave, and he arose and came out alive. It was that evidence that the people and Lazarus's sisters needed to witness to understand that both physical and spiritual life come from Christ through Christ's resurrection.

At such a young age, I would not have understood the reasons for the rejection nor would I have found peace in rejection. Sharing the Gospel is often challenging. Holding people, ourselves, and other Christians accountable to God's truth is hard, and rejection is surely to come. If I had received clarity or understanding then, I would never accept things I cannot change, and rejection just happens to be one of them. However, over the years, God has provided clarity to my rejection over the years. Where I once saw rejection was, in reality, God moving me closer to my purpose that I was to fulfill for him. This does not mean that rejection doesn't hurt or impact your life; it does mean that with time, you gain wisdom and perspective from the Lord enabling you to cope easier. The rejection that we sometimes face is either a time to grow and learn or a time that we are being removed from terrible situations that we are not able to fully see. We have to view these times as blessings from the Lord. For some reasons or another, those people or places were not going to be uplifting and encouraging to what God has in store for our future hope. However, with the clarity I did receive at the age of forty is rejection is not personal, it is not personal, it is fear of the truth, God's truth.

> *Jesus said to her, "I am the resurrection and life. Whoever believes in me, though he dies, yet shall he live, and everyone who lives and believes in me shall never die. Do you believe this?" (John 11:25–26 ESV)*

CHAPTER 4

Navigation of Loneliness When I'm not Alone

I am like a desert owl of the wilderness, like an owl of the waste places; I lie awake, I am like a lonely sparrow on the housetop. All the day my enemies taunt me; those who deride me use my name like a curse.

—Psalm 102:6–8 (ESV)

Let this be recorded for a generation to come, so that people yet to be created may praise the Lord; that he look down from his holy height, from heaven the Lord look down to Earth, to hear the groans of the prisoners, to set free those that were doomed to die, that they may declare in Zion thee name of the Lord, and in Jerusalem his praise, when peoples gather together, and kingdoms to worship the Lord.

—Psalm 102:18–21 (ESV)

Caroline was always the last person to get off the bus. Mrs. Elizabeth, her bus driver, would always give her the best advice and tell the greatest stories. She hated getting off that bus because she knew she was walking into an empty house that would remain that way until 6:00, 8:00, or even 10:00 p.m. If her mom was getting home early, meaning five-thirty, then she would have to have supper started. Caroline was cooking full meals by the time she was nine years old. Her lonely-days routine lasted for several years until she was fully into sports and finding her own rides home because her mother wouldn't be there, or she would wait in the high school parking lot after practice to sit in Oscar's truck. She would wait for Oscar to finish his sports or events so that they could go home. There was even a period or time when she became the manager of the wrestling team because she wasn't playing sports, and she was tired of being at home alone. Therefore, Caroline would go and watch Oscar's wrestling practice while waiting for him to get done, and the coach put her to work. Yes, for a girl growing up around boys all the time, she thought this was awesome because she felt as if she was finding her worth only through the attraction the older boys had for her. We all know teenage boys do not have the purest thoughts or desires for younger girls, but Caroline was finally feeling wanted and included. Caroline was never taught, told, or shown how to find her own worth and be happy with how God had made her.

Scripture tells us that we should find our identity in Christ. After her Mimi passed away, it seemed that not only were she and Oscar trying to find our identities, but also her mother had lost hers. Caroline helped me understand that for the majority of my childhood and young adult life, I was also searching to find my own identity. She helped me understand that trauma can cause a loss of focus on what God has for us, allowing open doors for demons and Satan to work tirelessly against us. It allows the search to fill the void in locations that are not good and pure but in sin and sinful behaviors. For me this type of behaviors made it extremely difficult for me because I was not getting the normal parental conversations that would help guide me to the appropriate source, God. It wasn't that my mother was lacking in these skills. She was still stuck in survival mode and would not get out of survival mode until I was grown and on our own. It just so happens that key times in my life, when I needed a mother to be a mother, I received a survivalist instead. Who can say that if faced with identical circumstances, I would not have reacted and maintained a survival mode until I was sure the sky wasn't falling? Well, Caroline confirmed that due to my own trauma experiences, I was living in survival mode, it may have been a bit different than the survival mode that my mother experienced, but it was still a survival mode. It was then that I realized that my survival mode was impacting my relationships with my own children, and to change that, I had to seek help and heal myself. Caroline has helped me see so much of my mother in myself that healing has taken a toll on me. I will say, however, that my identity became a survival identity because it was the only identity I experienced quality exposure to.

Therefore be imitators of God, and beloved children. And walk in love, as Christ loved us and gave himself for us, a fragrant offering and sacrifice to God. (Ephesians 5:1 ESV)

Be imitators of me, as I am of Christ. (1 Corinthians 11:1 ESV; Paul writing to the church of Corinth)

A year after Caroline's Mimi passed, her mom met a gentleman in Gatlinburg on a girl's weekend. Her mother needed that time away to help her with her mental health and self-care. Her mom was very lonely and needed a helpmate, and she had a constant desire to find Caroline and Oscar a father. She dated him long distance for around five to six months. The gentleman was from Georgia, and his name was Alex. When he would visit Caroline and her family, he would bring toys and such, to impress us. This was another one of those times that Caroline just couldn't place it, but something felt off, distant, as if she knew more than she realized. In the beginning, this gentleman seemed all nice and great, but that soon changed. Caroline and her family moved to Georgia, leaving all her friends, her best friend that had helped her through some of the worst times of her life, and now headed for a new one in Athens, Georgia.

Alex had a son that was just a year or two younger than Caroline. His name was Jacob. Jacob, of course, lived with his mother, so he wasn't very happy that there were new kids getting to spend more time with his dad than he was. Due to the custody agreement, he was only allowed over every other weekend and on Wednesdays. Alex's house was not all that big. Just two bedrooms, so Oscar and Jacob, of course, shared the second bedroom, with her mom and Alex being in the master, and Caroline was put into the laundry room, much like Cinderella. Now Caroline was told that the formal dining room would be made into a bedroom for her, but it actually became a storage area for all of her family belongings from their old life.

After the newness of the marriage wore off, Caroline could tell that Alex was not a big fan of girls or daughters. It may have been that he had never been around a lot of children that were girls and didn't know how to treat, comfort, act, or react with girls. There were times that he made an effort. He was really into baseball. He even coached her brother Oscar and Jacob on their different teams. He introduced Caroline to his aunt and encouraged her to play fast-pitch softball.

For Caroline, that separation or exclusion was still in the midst of her newfound family. She often found herself wandering across the street to her new step-grandmother's house or down the road to Alex's aunt's house. Many times, she felt like Cinderella because of always being pushed to the side for the boys; ultimately, Caroline would find ways to escape. Her love of reading grew even more prevalent. Reading gave her an escape from reality, and she could imagine another life for a while.

For the first time, her mother was a stay-at-home mom and had the opportunity to be a part of things that Caroline was doing at school and other activities. However, her mom chose not to. There was always an excuse she had to clean, cook supper, do some paperwork for Alex. It was very difficult for Caroline because she didn't understand it. In her eyes, she was seeing an opportunity that her mom was now being allowed to spend more time with her kids, and she was choosing to find some sort of work or something else to occupy her time. The close bonding between mother and daughter seemed as if it was never going to happen. Caroline longed so much to be close to her mother or really anyone. She made a few friends at school, but being the new kid, she was picked on and rejected. She did have a couple of sleepovers but no friends like she had in her previous life in North Carolina. She missed her home.

This marriage lasted only six months, and Caroline never really knew the truth or the details. She and Oscar were told that Alex had cheated on her mother and was physically abusing her. Her mom also explained that Alex was trying to get her mother to split her father's pension in three ways to include his son, Jacob. Each of these factors led to her decision to get a divorce. Oscar and Caroline do not recall any physical abuse or remember bruises or hearing verbal fighting. They just recalled one Saturday, when Alex was taking Jacob to a Braves Baseball Game, friends from North Carolina showed up with moving trucks, and they were to start packing because they were leaving that day. It was such a whirlwind experience for her. She really didn't know how to explain it. She didn't get to say goodbye to her newly made friends or her step-grandmother and step-grandfather that she had come to love due to spending so much time with them. Her family just woke up and left.

Once they got settled back in North Carolina, they lived with her aunt Marth and uncle Albert, who was her mother's brother. They had three kids, and Caroline and Oscar were close to them. Her mom began to get us reenrolled at their old schools. It was almost as if they were picking back up where they had left off. However, due to Caroline's absence for a little over six months, her friendships had started shifting, and she wasn't as close to her friends as she once was. Even her best friend and Caroline had started to drift apart. So the sense of loneliness began to sink in.

Caroline wasn't old enough to participate in school sports, her mom didn't want her staying with her granny; therefore, home alone became her solitude. It was these conversations with Caroline that I could most relate to. I think that is one of the main reasons that I have such a terrible time staying alone now. Boredom sets in; and that is when the devil likes to play with your thoughts, feelings, and emotions. Caroline's daily routines consisted of being the last to get off the school bus, coming inside, and calling her mother to let her know she was at home. If her mother didn't have school, work, or

FIGHTING DEMONS WHILE CHASING GOD!

a ball game of some sort to pick Oscar up from, then she would give Caroline instructions of when and how to start dinner. If she had school, work, or needed to pick up Oscar, then Caroline was on her own. It was around this time that she began watching TV for coping skills. The *I Love Lucy* show would come on every day at four and four thirty, then the five-o'clock news, and at five-thirty, *Andy Griffith Show*. On Wednesdays, every week, they would have an after-school special movie that would teach a lesson of some sort on drugs, dating, sex, teen pregnancy, etc. Depending if she was cooking dinner, the remainder of the evening was finding something to eat, working on her homework if she had any, and watching TV, taking a shower, then reading a while before going to sleep.

When her mother and Oscar would come in, they would either talk in another room or Oscar would retreat to his room to play video games. They never sat at the kitchen or dining room table to eat together. They would just fix a plate and come to the living room and watch TV while they would eat. It was Oscar or Caroline's chore to clean the kitchen, while their mother would retreat to her room to be alone. On a few occasions, their mother would stay and hangout with them. Those nights, after we had gone to bed, Caroline would hear her playing the piano. Classical music was the only music she knew how to play. It would become a moment in time where Caroline felt a true sense of peace, love, and security within her home.

Not long after returning back to her life in North Carolina, her mom tried her hand at dating again because she needed someone and hated being alone. She also felt the need to find Caroline and Oscar a father. Her uncle Albert set her up with a fellow coworker that worked with him. His name was Sam. He would sometimes spend the night or stay well after Caroline and Oscar had gone to bed. Every now and then, he would show up to the house before Caroline's mother would get home, but it would be only a few minutes.

It was just about this time when her life was finally starting to settle down that it was time to face yet another demon, one of predatory nature. Here Caroline was, a lonely young girl, just wanting attention from anyone, and finally her mother had met a guy that was now nice to me as well, not just Oscar. One Wednesday afternoon, Caroline got off the bus at four o'clock and came in, called her mother like she told her to. Her mother instructed Caroline to be quiet because Sam was there sleeping before his shift at work. Repairmen were working at his apartment or something. This is a time in Caroline's recollection that became hard to remember every detail. She explained that in her own life, it has become hard to remember every detail, but the details she did remember were terrifying and painful. It is funny what the memory does to protect its own mental capacity. Caroline remembered that she was instructed to be extra quiet and not bother Sam and that her mother would be home later. She stated that Caroline could not watch TV because the living room was right under her bedroom, and the sound would travel up and wake him up. So she was left to find something in my room to keep her quiet. This is what she was trying to do.

A short while later, she heard Sam get up and heard the water running in her mother's bathroom. So she just assumed he was taking a shower. She decided to stay in my room, doing her homework and reading, waiting for Sam to get up and leave so she could go watch TV. He finally came to Caroline's room and asked if she wanted to hangout and watch TV with him. Caroline was surprised but thought, okay, cool, someone actually wanting to spend time with her. She went downstairs to watch TV, but he suggested that they watch in her mother's room, in case he fell back asleep so he could be comfortable. Unknowingly, Caroline agreed and thought how cool is it that finally her mother had found someone that liked her for her and was ready to be her dad. She was feeling really loved and wanted at the time. She even got a secure feeling of maybe this might even be the changing point in her life when things start to get better.

Sam and Caroline went into her mother's room and climbed onto the bed, propping the pillows up to lean on, and watched TV. He asked what she liked to watch, and she told him that it was Wednesday, so that is normally when the after-school specials come on and suggested that they watch that. He agreed, and they sat there for a few minutes. He asked if she was comfortable, and she was, and he said, "That's good," and put his arm around her. At first, she thought, *This man really cares about me. How awesome*. It was then that the mood and feelings she began to have went from excited that she finally have a male figure that wants me as a daughter to what is happening? This man wants her in a sexual way, and that is not cool.

As they sat there with his hand on her shoulder, he seemed to relax his hand in a manner that it was barely laying on her breast area. At first, she wasn't sure what to do. Was this an accident? Or was something else going on? She began to become uncomfortable, so she slid away a bit, making him have to adjust his arm from around her shoulders. They sat there a while longer, and he began to rub her leg, telling her how great it was to get to spend quality time with her and to really get to know her. That, too, began to make Caroline feel even more uncomfortable, but what was she supposed to do? This man was a friend of Uncle Albert, her mom's boyfriend. Could she be imagining all of this? She told herself that she was reading way more into it than it was and to just relax and watch the show. A few moments later, his hand went from the top of her thigh to her lower stomach and then to her private parts. He went to go to the buttons of her pants, but Caroline began to freak out and jumped up and ran to her room and locked the door.

A short while later, he came and knocked on her door to see if she was okay and to let her know he was leaving. Caroline just sat up on her bed and didn't say a word. She heard him leave and pull out of the driveway. It didn't matter; at that moment, she was so scared that she stayed in her room until her mother got home. She got home and knocked on Caroline's door and asked why she watched TV after she told her not to, that she had woke Sam up. She sat there dumbfounded and couldn't respond. Caroline ended up being grounded for a week, which meant she couldn't have any friends over and would not be allowed to go and stay with friends. The whole while Caroline could not get off her bed and unlock the door because her mother was mad, Caroline was scared and didn't know what to say or how to tell her because Sam had lied and told her that she came home and started watching TV and woke him up. Caroline took the punishment and didn't speak of that day to anyone until about a year later, when she wrote about it in an essay for her seventh-grade English class. Even when the essay was given to her mom, she didn't believe Caroline. Her mother felt that she had written it because of the tension and disagreements that were occurring between her and Caroline. Her mother felt like Caroline was trying to make her look like a bad mother. It was never addressed again. This incident left a lasting weary impression on men and guys in general on Caroline. She immediately put a guard up when it came to anyone that wanted to date her mother.

For the remainder of their relationship, Caroline kept a big distance from Sam, and her mom always wondered why she was acting weird around him. Needless to say, it wasn't much longer after that Sam and Caroline's mother broke it off. Caroline's mother caught him cheating on her with a younger girl too. It seemed like all the guys that wanted to date her mother were never good enough or were always out for money or something that they shouldn't be after. Looking back, the men that she dated were never really interested in the best interest of her, Oscar, and Caroline. She said she always felt that they were the victim's family. Something always bad was happening to them. She said it seemed they could never catch a break. I know that I could relate to that concept. It seems that I myself have always seemed to be waiting for the other shoe to drop. Doomsday is right around the corner.

Understanding that different members of trauma experiences internalize things differently because the same trauma is absorbed from different perspectives. Having one person coming to grips and healing or being okay with the trauma experience doesn't always mean that everyone who experienced the trauma is okay. That is why depending on God to be the comforter and healer is crucial in surviving traumatic experiences. Unfortunately, I never knew how my brother or mother handled all of the same experiences. Our family never really talked about our feelings or how things made us feel. It was as if we could never connect. It was almost as though we cohabitated in the same trauma experiences but never discussed what damage the trauma was causing. There always seemed to be an obstacle in our way, whether it was sports, our genders, friends, Momma, or even the simple fact we were facing the same obstacles without leaning on each other for help. It was almost like a silent command that we were not allowed to just talk about what was happening to us. Many times, we didn't feel like a family. We felt like three people living in a house together.

Often, we as Christians just simply go through the motions. We attend church, give our tithes, and perform good deeds, but actions are not what solidifies our relationship. We have to make a concerted effort. Communication is the key. You have to want to know God's desires. He already wants to know ours and does know ours. The difference is He wants us as His children to have the desire to tell Him. He wants us to freely share our innermost desires, concerns, dreams, fears—all with Him on a level that is more than just a head knowledge of routine and motions, but with a heart knowledge of who Christ Jesus is as our Savior and Lord.

During these times in my life, I would often wonder where God was and why I feel all alone. Often there are times in everyone's life that we feel that we are alone or that no one can relate to what we are going through. I find that is when the attributes of Christ should begin to shine through us as Christians. Holding fast to the words of truth, the Word of God is what can grant direction during the loneliness that we feel so desperately at times.

Psalm 25:4 says, "Make your ways known to me, Lord, teach me your paths." Even the servant David felt moments of loneliness and despair that he questioned God and His will, not in a way without gratitude, but in a way of desiring wisdom and understanding for the trials and struggles with the enemy he was facing. Further along, in Psalm 27:7–10, David continues to cry out for understanding and clarity.

> Lord, hear my voice when I call: be gracious to me and answer me. My heart says this about you: "Seek his face." Lord, I will seek your face. Do not hide your face from me; do not turn your servant away in anger; You have been my helper; do not leave me or abandon me, God is my Salvation. Even if my father and mother abandon me, the Lord cares for me. (Psalm 27:7–10 ESV)

In search for the Lord, David knew that he would never really be alone because if he was truly seeking God, then God would reveal Himself to David in his time of need and comfort. During my times of loneliness, I found comfort in reading books, school and learning, recreational sports, and those individuals that coached those sports because they worked with me. It seems that they saw potential in me. They saw something in me and encouraged that growth, whether it be in learning or athletics. I feel that they saw so much more in me than I had ever imagined. Sometimes, I feel those few key figures in my life that had huge impacts saw the seeds that God had planted growing, and they began to nurture them for my emotional and spiritual growth that I needed at that time. God loves us so much that He provides comfort when we need comfort, strength when we need strength, and companionship when we need a friend.

CHAPTER 5

From Child to Parent

Beloved, do not be surprised at the fiery trial when it comes upon you to test you, as though something strange were happening to you. But rejoice insofar as you share Christ's sufferings, that you may also rejoice and be glad when his glory is revealed. If you are insulted in the name of Christ then you are blessed because the Spirit of glory and of God rests upon you.

—1 Peter 4:12–14 (ESV)

After you have suffered a little while, the God of all grace, who has called you to his eternal glory will himself restore, confirm, strengthen, and establish you.

—1 Peter 5:10 (ESV)

Shortly after Caroline's mother's relationship ended with Sam, she dated a few other men, one that she met and worked with. His name was Carl. Caroline remembers meeting Carl once when she was at her mom's workplace but was introduced as a coworker. Caroline was struggling with her mother's need to have someone else in her life when she and Oscar were there for her. She recalls that oftentimes, her mother was mesmerized by him to the point that she picked her and her best friend up from one of her basketball games to go and ride by Carl's house. Caroline and her friend wanted to stay and watch the boys play, but her mother insisted that she had somewhere that she needed to be. Even though this was the time Caroline was getting to spend with her mother, it was not the quality time that a daughter dreams of spending with her mother. It is interesting how the flesh can often overcome the rational and righteousness of God.

There are many tactics that Satan uses to distract us from the plan God has for our lives. That is why it is so important to study the scriptures and arm yourself in the full armor of God that is found in Ephesians 6:11–19 (ESV).

> Put on the full armor of God, so that you will be able to stand firm against the schemes of the devil. For our struggle is not against flesh and blood, but against the rulers, against the powers, against the world forces of this darkness, against the spiritual forces of wickedness in the heavenly places.

Therefore, take up the full armor of God so that you will be able to resist the evil day, and having done everything, stand firm. Stand firm; therefore, *have your loins girded with truth*, *put on the breastplate of righteousness*, and *shod your feet with the preparation of the gospel of peace*. In addition to all, take up the shield of faith with which you will be able to extinguish all the flaming arrows of the evil one and take *the helmet of salvation* and the sword of the Spirit, which is the Word of God. With all prayer and petition, pray at all times in the Spirit, and with this in view, be on the alert with all perseverance and petition for all the saints, and pray on my behalf that utterance may be given to me in the opening of my mouth, to make known with boldness the mystery of the gospel.

Since Caroline was not allowed in private conversations with her brother and mother, the only way she knew about the details of that relationship was to eavesdrop on phone calls during the late night. She only listened a few times due to curiosity and because she wanted to understand what was so intriguing that was taking her mother's attention away from her and Oscar. The main thing that Caroline got from those conversations was that her mother was so in love with Carl and so hurt that he would not leave his wife to be with her. When they finally called it quits, it led to major depression and struggles for her mother.

In such a short time span, her mother had broken things off with Carl, had a sexual harassment lawsuit at work, making her need to find another job, all of which put an enormous amount of stress and pressure on her to provide for Caroline and Oscar. Her brother, Oscar, was beginning to drive and needed a vehicle. His driving experience, to begin with, was not very great. He had several tickets and a couple of wrecks. This also added bills and stress to her mother because it was a help and benefit to have Oscar driving Caroline and himself back and forth to school, sporting events, and practice. During this time, loneliness crept into Caroline's family, and each of them was beginning to seclude themselves in a way that was detrimental to their health. School and sports activities were a great distraction for Caroline and Oscar. However, for her mother, the enemy came at her hard and viciously. With all the added stress and loneliness that began to overtake her, she became very depressed, so depressed that her daily routines became that she would get up for work, go to work, and come straight home, and go to bed. There were months to almost a year that she did this every day. If she had any contact with Caroline or her brother, it was to fuss about chores or to just express her anger at the world, and unfortunately, the children seemed to be her sounding boards. Caroline admitted that she often felt she was more of a sounding board because she did not have a way out or away.

Through the many conversations that I have had with Caroline, the way I could relate to her and her experiences were parallel. Depression can impact so many individuals differently. I know for myself there would be times when my brother and I would beg our mother to fix something for us to eat. It was then when the excuses would always come. Realizing that depression had taken hold time seemed to not register with her, we would be out of groceries for days or weeks, and she never realized the magnitude of her distress and the huge impact that her stress and absence had on me and my brother. Caroline explained to me that depression can be one of the worst enemies or demons that many individuals fight. What individuals need to understand is the stigma of therapy and mental health issues, even depression, hindered so many individuals from getting the help that they deserved and needed, when it shouldn't hinder them. God has been gracious enough to allow the minds to work wonders with repression and forgetting particular painful periods of our lives. Caroline has explained this is a way for the brain and body to protect itself from reliving painful periods, thus creating imaginary memories that are more conducive to not stressing the body. When my brother and I mention our childhood years around our mother, our memories and her memories do not always align, and I feel that is because our childhood occurred during her most painful times, to protect her, God allowed her to repress those memories so that she could survive to take care of us.

In Caroline's family, she expressed her concern for her mother's depression and isolation process had gone on so long that the seriousness of her condition had not registered to anyone within their family. One early morning, Caroline remembered having to grab something out of her mother's bathroom and her mother stepped out of the shower, and it was Caroline's face that said it all. Caroline's only description was her mother looked like one of the starving children or individuals from a Third World country. She believed the look on her face made her mother realize that it was bad. From that point forward, roles shifted in Caroline's family. She became the forceful parent that had to start getting her mother thick whole milk or heavy cream chocolate shakes with raw eggs put in them. This was to help her mother gain some immediate weight and fast. Caroline's mother had begun to literally starve herself to death, and according to the doctor, she was not that far from dying. Due to the depression and isolation, Caroline not only explained the trauma of loneliness but also now had to assume an adult role of taking care and providing for her mother. The amount of stress and trauma that was inflicted on Caroline was yet another maneuver from the enemy to deter Caroline from seeking strength and mercy from the Lord.

FIGHTING DEMONS WHILE CHASING GOD!

Caroline would get off the school bus and prepare dinner. After getting her mother to the table, she would not allow her to leave the table until her mother had cleaned her plate. This role for Caroline became as she was the one becoming the parent, making sure that her mother had all the nutrients that she needed and was actually eating. Caroline constantly checked after her mother, making sure she was taking the required vitamins to get her back to being physically able to live. Caroline admitted that at times, it was very frustrating and scary and, a lot of the times, made her very angry that she was having to take the role of the parent when so many times prior she had needed a parent and didn't feel as if she had what she needed as a parent.

Often, during these times, Caroline's mother would find things that she would accuse her of and refuse to believe Caroline, no matter what she says, which would infuriate Caroline even further. For example, her family had to have some men come in and work on the heating and air conditioning system, which ran up through Caroline's closet. Caroline admitted that her closet was small, and she was not the best at organizing. Most of the time, her room was never the tidiest, but really, what teenager doesn't go through the stage of tossing everything in the closet and under the bed? One day, when Caroline's mother was feeling up to doing some laundry while the kids were at school, she went to put the items up in Caroline's closet and found a couple of unsmoked cigarettes in her closet. When Caroline arrived home, her mother went off the deep end, accusing her of smoking. This made Caroline so mad when she explained that it probably fell out of one of the men's pockets when they were working on the HVAC system. The men came to work on the HVAC system when her mother was so depressed and was isolating herself in her room. However, that explanation didn't seem rational to her. It was her daughter doing something terrible that seemed more realistic. The only proper solution was her fourteen-year-old daughter had started smoking, and since she came to that conclusion, it was the truth despite Caroline's pleas and begging that there was no truth to that assumption.

The anger that came over Caroline from these accusations was unreal. She explained the experience as if demons were trying to possess her. She detailed the experience as a feeling of anger came from places that had nothing to do with the accusations. The thoughts that were running through her mind were similar to "you haven't been around or aware of what Oscar and I have been doing for the past year, what gives you the right to step in now?" This is a time for Caroline who has stepped in as a parental role, ensuring that her mother is getting the nourishment that she needs to stay alive, be a teenage girl facing all the girl drama at school with no motherly guidance, and now accusations from the very person she has been fighting to keep alive. I must admit, when I put myself in Caroline's shoes, I understood the anger, hurt, and trauma that she was feeling. But being an outsider looking in, it is almost as if her mother wasn't her mother but demon-possessed; Caroline was facing a spiritual battle that she had never seen before.

The enemy or Satan was using the flesh of her mother to play roles of anger and depression by making her choose the times she would decide to be a parent and when she wanted to be depressed and check out of her role as a parent. Caroline expressed how she always felt like the times that her mother chose to be a parent were crappy decisions and unjust decisions. Caroline explained that her mother knew she had never liked the smell of smoke, being around smoke, and was not friends with anyone that did smoke, so her first question to her mother was, where did she think that she got them? Second question: Did her mother not realize that Caroline hadn't had time to spend with her friends other than at school because she had become a caregiver to her mother? Caroline had taken it upon herself to take care of her mother ensuring that she would live. Third question: that Caroline had for her mother was where does she get the nerve to decide to be a part of my life when, the last six months to a year, she could have cared less what Oscar or she was doing because her mother was so depressed and had isolated herself in her bedroom. There were many times that Caroline had noted that her mother didn't even know if her kids were eating or had groceries to eat when, many times, they didn't, and Oscar would beg her to get up and go get groceries.

FIGHTING DEMONS WHILE CHASING GOD!

It is amazing what the enemy will use against you and your loved ones to ensure that God does not receive the glory He deserves. This story provided to me by Caroline was a perfect example of the enemy using her mother's pain, depression, and loneliness to destroy the seeds that God had already established in Caroline's life. At this point in her life, she was just learning and understanding that her mother was all she truly had here on earth. She was her defender, her provider, her authority, my keeper, her protector, and in this situation, her enemy. Satan can often use those closest to us to tear away our faith and trust in the Lord to provide and protect. If Satan could get Caroline to be angry or hate or turn away from what God had provided her as her parental figure, then he could also get her to turn her faith away from God as a Provider, Protector, Authority Figure, Defender, Keeper, and Savior. Looking back, Caroline realized it was a strong tactic that Satan is trying to capitalize on even today, destroying the family. I have to agree with her. I experienced similar situations with my own family, even though my family was just a mother, brother, and me, but it was my family. There are times, even now, when I see the tactics of Satan and demons trying to cause issues within my family. I have often wondered what it would be like if I just walked away and what is the biblical context of that. I had a very wise person tell me once that you must be kind to all those that you can and leave the rest of them alone. I have often wondered if it was the right thing to do, but in scripture, Jesus either lets or walks away from individuals who refuse to believe in him and his ministry forty-one different times. I suppose if Christ can let people walk away or walk away from people, then so can I.

The thing is Satan started plotting to destroy me many years ago when my dad died, and there had been times he was so close to completely destroying me, but God. I have read several times that if you are getting attacked by Satan, hard and often, it is because he does not want you to reach the potential and will God has for your life. Thieves do not break into empty houses, so Satan knew that something strong had already set root in my life, even if it had not started shining through.

Genesis 3:1 says, "Now the serpent was more crafty than any other beasts of the field that the Lord God had made. He said to the Woman, 'Did God actually say, You shall not eat of any tree in the garden?'" Satan began attacking the family from the very beginning.

Through many years, I have been accused of being deceitful, worthless, "not going to account to anything," lazy, and rebellious, numerous times, by my own mother. Words were her weapon that the enemy allowed her to use against me to tear down what God was building up. Caroline explained that she and her brother endured being verbally attacked for not honoring their mother for years even into adulthood, or accused of not loving her. Caroline explained that her mother was very good at using her words to get individuals to the point of doing exactly what she wanted because that individual would be so broken down that they would do something that was completely against their beliefs to avoid a fight. Caroline admitted that Oscar has become so much better at avoiding an argument than she ever did. She explained that she had some fights in her. God had granted her the will to stand her ground and, even to this day, she will stand my ground, most of the time, she said it had been to her detriment. She has often asked God why He put that fight for what is right and good in her heart. That is a question we should all be asking to have that desire in our hearts. However, many of us would rather stay on the sidelines and allow others to be bold and courageous to stand up for God and what is just and right. I often wonder if this is what the enemy sees and is trying to stop in many of us.

Some of the conclusions that I have been able to come to with spending time with Caroline is that I know that my mother loves me; however, I also know that pain, loneliness, and frustration can also make you say and do things that are unfathomable to your children. Due to my childhood trauma, pain, and emotional roller coaster rides that I have experienced, with my very own mother, I, unfortunately, said similar things to my own kids as they were younger, which were completely unfair and unjust to my own children. Over the past few years, I had not had the best relationship with my two oldest children, so on the day after Christmas, I decided they were going to get off their chest what I had done or said to them to make them so guarded around me and not as close to me as my youngest two children were. Talking about facing your demons, I had to face my own demons that I had inflicted onto my own children. It was brutal. No mother wants to sit, hear, and truly listen to all the bad things they had done and failed their children as a mother. But I knew if I wanted any shot at a relationship with my children that I would cherish, I had to do it.

It was the hardest moment as a mother, I think, that I ever had to endure. I do believe that my heart was completely ripped out of my chest repeatedly; however, it was the best thing I could have done for my children. I gave them a voice. I owned my mistakes and took accountability for my actions. I sought God's help to learn and grow from them and to help build better relationships with my children.

Proverbs 4:23 states, "Keep your heart with all vigilance, for from it flows the springs of life."

Growing up in an atmosphere that was never good enough or not always encouraging calloused my heart with painful words that I carried over to my children. When I sat and listened to them explain how I had hurt them and made them feel, I knew they were being honest and telling the truth because I also saw myself sitting right there with them, expressing the same hurt and disappointment. Unfortunately, my own mother has never, and sadly, I never see her being willing to hear my voice the same way. I pray that it is not too late, but the time and the fight that I have deep within me knows that there is far more damage that needs repairing than the damage I had with my own children. That is why we as Christians must be so diligent to protect our heart, where the Holy Spirit dwells, because the enemy will use loved ones to kill, steal, and destroy us. I knew that if I was going to emotionally heal for myself, I had to stop the emotional roller coaster that I was on and stop the traumatic cycle of passing forward pain that I could not prevent through emotionally verbally hurting my kids.

Please don't take this as I was never verbally or emotionally hurtful to my mother. I learned how to use words as vengeful painful attacks from the example I was given. Similar to Caroline, I am a fighter. Unfortunately, I have learned how to fight back really well with words, and that is something that I am not proud of, but I am trying and praying that God will fix that within me. I would love to make amends with my mother, but it will take time, mutual understanding and respect, and the emotional intelligence that is capable of owning our mistakes. That is where the wonderful opportunity of forgiveness comes into play. God is the perfect model of forgiveness, grace, and mercy. It is God's unconditional love that He not only wants to forgive us, show us mercy but to also provide grace. He forgives us when we admit that we are sinners and cannot make it through life or eternity without Him. He demonstrates mercy when He does not rain down His wrath of hell on us. He provided grace through the gift of salvation, by sacrificing His only Son to take on the punishment of every human's sin. Whether we accept Him or not, He has already suffered our punishment. It brings me to tears to think of that because what have I done to deserve that when, even as I try my hardest to live an upright and righteous life, I still fall short daily? That is when I know, without a shadow of doubt, whatever demon I face, my God is bigger and greater than any demon that the enemy can send my way.

CHAPTER 6

Searching to Belong and to Be Loved

The plans of the heart belong to man, but the answer from the tongue is from the Lord. All the ways of man are pure in his own eyes, but the Lord weighs the spirit. Commit your work to the Lord and your plans will be established. The Lord has made everything for its purpose, even the wicked for the day of trouble.

—Proverbs 16:1–4 (ESV)

For the next few years, Caroline lived your typical teenage years with the exception she started working and providing, spending money and buying her own wardrobe when she was fourteen years old. As a student, she maintained As and Bs, played sports, and joined as many clubs as she could. Even though she had a relationship with Christ, there was still a part of her searching to be included, belonged, and loved. Church during these years went back to being scattered here and there, so her own growth with the Lord came in small spurts. She knew what right and wrong was. She had already started establishing her own morals and how she wanted to treat other people. Most individuals have begun to find their identities at that age, but unfortunately, Caroline was still searching. She knew that she was a child of God, but at that time in her life, she needed something tangible. What she didn't realize is even though God was not a physical being right in front of her, he was more tangible than ever. She hadn't learned how to see him in the tangible things around her, like the sunset, the changing fall leaves, the new growth in spring, the unexpected people that popped into her life, and the gifts in the individuals who supported her. Often I explained to Caroline that I found myself wanting something tangible and forgot to have gratitude for the small blessings and tangible things God was already providing me. I suppose that is the case with many of us; unfortunately, many of us never gain that gratitude.

By the time she started high school, she began realizing that several of her friends were not truly her friends unless she benefitted them in some way. Caroline and I agree on that demon, that many times we see that the real world works this way often. I explained to Caroline that I was told by a very special lady that you have only four to five close true friends throughout your life if you are lucky. At first, I didn't believe that concept, but Caroline agreed that she had learned that lesson the hard way, and it became a huge eye-opener for her. Her close girl friendships were scarce, and the relationships that she sought out with different guys who she thought were genuinely good guys, and eventually grew up to be good guys, were not great guys in high school. Caroline was pretty and popular, and therefore, guys normally didn't like her for the same reasons she liked them.

She would endure time and time again rejection from being included in various activities with groups of friends, rejection from her mother not making true efforts to come and support her in her sporting events. There were even times when she would attend events on weekends or at summer camps. A parent night was a normal part of the event, and she would often receive excuses of not being able to go, then return home to see if the excuse she was given was just now being started or done. Caroline began receiving rejection from my brother not wanting her to be around him or his friends because he would get picked on, and rejection from guys when she would not cave to peer pressure. This type of rejection gave way to a deep feeling of worthlessness, never being good enough for her friend group, her mother, her brother, and guys. I understand that everyone has these types of experiences throughout their lives, but what that does to an individual internally begins to create someone that becomes a people pleaser, losing a part of themselves in order to please people enough to be included or feel some sort of value. I myself had become a people pleaser. Caroline helped me realize that my own self-worth had been shattered as a child and that the only way I was understood to get approval, inclusion, or appreciation was to only do what others wanted while sacrificing myself and my own desires. That was a lesson that I had to learn, and I have had to make very difficult decisions to change and build my own self-worth back up to the value that God values me. I explained to Caroline that all that I wanted was to feel like someone cared, comforted, and celebrated when something good happened—close to someone who was excited that I was a part of their world. She helped me understand that all I was longing for and desiring, God was preparing for me in the family that he would one day give me, the family that I prayed for—big, happy, close, and loving. God always keeps his promises, and he blessed me with the most wonderful loving husband who supports me beyond belief and four beautiful healthy children. What makes it even more precious is God is bringing God-fearing partners into their lives to grow and build their own families, which has made me so proud. It is another example. As I was fighting demons of loneliness, worthlessness, and finding inclusion, Caroline helped me realize that God was taking note of what I would need to ensure I had a prosperous and expected end, just like in the scripture *Jeremiah 29:11*, which states, *"For I know the plans that I have for you,' declares the* LORD, *'plans for welfare and not for calamity to give you a future and a hope.'"*

Sometimes, it takes someone else who has had similar experiences to help you recognize God's plan and fight for your well-being. Even though my trials and battles had been similar to Caroline's, it was her help that allowed me to work through the next battle with the demon of death.

After I had dated a few jerks, God brought someone into my life to teach me what it felt like to truly be loved. His name was Derrick. It was the end of my junior year. One of my friends, Tracy, and her family were building a new house, and I went to go see it with her. It just so happened that the brick masons were there, and that is where I met Derrick. He was so handsome and shy. It was funny how his coworkers (which were his uncles) teased him to get my number. Finally, as I was getting ready to leave, he quickly asked for my number, so I gave it to him. Surprisingly, he called that evening. We decided to set up a double date with my brother and his new wife because Derrick had graduated with my brother, Wayne. Derrick and I fell in love immediately. At first, I was concerned that it was infatuation, but it wasn't. He was just as crazy about me, if not more so than I was about him. We began to see each other every day.

It was just three weeks, and school was soon over, allowing us lots of time to spend together every evening, when he would get off work. My mom had finally remarried and was living her best life as a newlywed, so she really didn't pay much attention or care where I was or what I was doing. My brother had also gotten married the day before my mother, out of haste, due to an argument that he and my mother had gotten into. The timing of this relationship with Derrick was completely in God's plan because He knew that I needed to feel true love if I would ever be able to recognize it. God also knew that I had been yearning for it for a long time, and my mother was becoming more and more preoccupied with her own relationship, therefore ignoring me. Wayne was also becoming more and more involved in his relationship, and I was becoming more and more lonely. Our relationship lasted only two months, but they were some of the best two months of my life.

It is funny that when God provides blessings, and you begin to grow closer toward Him, the enemy begins to work in overdrive. During those two months, I really didn't have many arguments with my mother. I was doing well at work, and I was enjoying getting to know Derrick. He was a brick mason and farmer. I would often go over to his house, and we would ride around and feed the cows, visit with his mom and dad, or go swimming. If I didn't get to see him, we would stay up late, talking on the phone. Once school let out, I would often meet him for lunch. One thing that I used to think was so funny is that Derrick would anticipate my every move. He could read me like a book, which I thought was amazing because I had never had a guy pay that much attention to me. Reflecting now, I realize that God was teaching me how to see my own worth because there were others who saw my worth like God intended it to be seen. There were so many lessons that I reflect back on that God taught me through and with Derrick that I can only say those two months brought me such joy, happiness, and love that I had never really felt or don't recall feeling. It was getting close to his birthday, and his friends wanted to take him to the beach. I knew that I was going to miss him, but I thought, *Okay, no big deal, a guy has to have his guy time.* It just so happened his birthday fell on June 29, which meant he would be at the beach for the week of July Fourth. I knew I would miss him, but I would survive.

I hate gut feelings. So far, they have always been right for me. While he was at the beach, I was at work and had to call his mother because, all of a sudden, I got an enormous weird sick feeling that something was wrong, and Derrick was hurt. I called his mom, and she reassured me that everything was okay. The call did settle my nerves, but when he got home, I had the feeling again and broke down and cried about it to him. I know he probably thought I was crazy, but I had to tell him. It felt too much like the time when a similar sick feeling the day my father died.

The day he came home, I had already arrived at his house and was swimming in the pool, waiting on him to get there. I couldn't wait to see him. Once he arrived, his mom went and talked him a bit, and then I came over to see him, and he had went shopping and bought me all kinds of clothes. He showed me a polaroid picture that the guys had taken of him on the phone, talking to me, instead of partying it up with them. I had never had a guy do this for me. I knew then that he loved me more than anything. We continued to enjoy our time together, whether working on the tractor, picking up rocks out of the field, fishing, riding around the cow pastures, or laying in the back of his truck, counting the stars and talking. It all had become so magical. Then death showed his horrific presence again in my life.

July eleventh, we had gone out on a date and went back to his house to make brownies and go fishing. The sun had been so hot that day, and he was extremely tired from working in the heat. His mom offered to take me home since I lived forty-five minutes away.

He said no, and that he would stop and get coffee if he needed it. He took me home and was trying to fall asleep in my driveway. I tried and tried to get him to come in and at least take a small nap on the couch before he had to drive all the way back to Jackson Creek. Derrick was such a gentleman. He would not want anyone to think bad of me if he was to stay. I finally kissed him good night, and he left very tired. I promised I would call him in about an hour to make sure he got home okay. I went upstairs and wrote in my diary (which was weird. It was the only time I kept a diary, and it was only of our relationship).

I fell asleep and didn't call Derrick; however, I was awakened by the phone ringing round 12:30 a.m. It was his best friend, Jeff. Half asleep, I answered the phone. Jeff was asking, "Where is Derrick? What time did he leave your house?"

I was trying to answer his questions, all the while frustrated with myself for falling asleep. Then Jeff said, "Faith, there has been a wreck, and it looks like Derrick's. I'm going to try to get closer and check, and I'll call you back."

I immediately hung up and started calling Derrick's grandma's house because he stayed with her at night because she was deaf and lived alone. No answer. Nothing. Fear began to set in. Jeff called back, and I answered the phone. He told me that it was Derrick's truck, and that I needed to get to the hospital because it did not look good. By this time, the phone calls had awoken my mother, and I told her what was going on. She began getting dressed, and my stepdad, being a deputy sheriff, put in a call. I had never gotten dressed so fast in my life. I was sitting at the top of the steps, waiting on my mom, just rocking, saying that everything was going to be okay. It is not that bad. Mom came out of the bedroom and told me that I needed to be brave and strong and prepare myself for the worse. I told her no, that he was fine. We got in the car and drove to the hospital in silence.

Once I arrived at the hospital, Jeff met me at the door, and I could tell he was upset. He said, "Faith, it isn't good," and he just held me for a few minutes. Then he took me to the room that Derrick's parents and aunt and uncle were in. Shortly, thereafter, the state trooper came in and had Derrick's wallet and belongings. I crumbled and walked out and between Jeff and my mother holding me up. We walked to my mom's car and then went to Derrick's house. I was in a state of unbelief, numb, and shock, not fully understanding that my life had just came face to face with the demon of death yet again. It was a so kinda real thing. He had died exactly like my father had. I was beside myself.

Over the next few days, it was a blur. I sat in with his parents and planned my first funeral at the age of seventeen years old. I picked out his clothes, his flowers, the memory verses, casket, and times of the funeral. It was so real and yet felt like a living nightmare. The night that the family gathered at the funeral home, everyone went back to Derrick's house, and I stayed the night again. I hadn't slept in about two days, but I didn't want to fall asleep alone. Jeff and Garrett, Derrick's friends, sat in his room until I went to sleep. Then the heavenly experience that I felt was amazing. I had a dream about Derrick walking in a field, then behind his house, in his backyard. I literally woke myself up, reaching out for him. He was smiling, and he kept saying to me, "Faith, it is all going to be okay." He repeated that several times before I woke up, reaching for him. God gave me closure and reassurance all in that one dream.

Not only did I have to fight the demon of death, but now I was going to have demons of depression, loneliness, hopelessness, doubt, grief, anger, all while trying to find the will to live. These feelings lasted for several months after Derrick's death; however, God was already working on His master plan.

Shortly after Derrick's death, I will never forget, one evening, while at work, my seventh grade math teacher, Mrs. McDowell, came in to see me and gave me a card that had the following scripture on it. It was the first time that I began to connect the dots that scripture can be healing, comforting, and true. Jeremiah 29:11 states:

> *For I know the plans I have for you, declares the Lord, plans for welfare and not for evil, to give you a future and a hope. (ESV)*

"For I know the plans I have for you," declares the Lord, "plans to prosper you and not to harm you, plans to give you hope and a future. (NIV)

For I know the thoughts that I think toward you, says the Lord, thoughts of peace and not of evil, to give you a future and a hope. (NKJV)

For I know the thoughts that I think toward you, saith the Lord, thoughts of peace and not of evil, to give you an expected end. (KJV)

I searched through several versions of the scripture to truly understand what God was trying to tell me and really what inspiration my seventh grade teacher, who I had not seen in years, came out to share with me. My interpretation of this was it was all a part of God's grand plan for my life, and although I was hurting and grieving, now it was to grant me a more prosperous, peaceful, future full of hope. Due to my pain being so big and raw at the moment, I found only a minor bit of comfort, but it was the first comfort that I had felt in a long time.

I think that during the funeral and all the people that reached out to me, my mother had realized there was a big part of me that she did not know because she had been focused on her life and happiness. For a while, she became the mother I had longed for all my life. However, there were still times she knew how to use her words of anger and manipulation to bring perspective back to your mind that she was queen bee, and your life was not your own. It was hers to dictate what would be done with it. If anyone can master the art of manipulation with words and get you to do what they want, all the while making you feel as if it were your decision, that would be my mother or she would just guilt you into submission that you would soon avoid the guilt trip or manipulation altogether.

Sometimes, I often wonder how long do we as hurt individuals continue to hurt those closest to us when God has made a way out of the painful or destructive situations we were in? I know for me, and I feel also my mother, holding on to pain can often become a security blanket because we are always ready for the next attack that we forget to see the blessings that are right in front of us. When individuals, and even Christians, have been through so many painful situations, they begin to live in fight-or-flight mode constantly. Reaction time becomes impeccable to the point we are so reactive we miss God's grace, along with His peace and rest that He provides us.

"There is one whose rash words are like sword thrusts, but the tongue of the wise brings healing" (Proverbs 12:18 ESV).

"Therefore, confess your sins to one another and pray for one another, that you may be healed. The prayer of a righteous person has great power as it is working" (James 5:16 ESV).

Stepping out of the repeated trauma cycle can be hard, especially if you have battled all through life with the same individual, embracing the concepts that others are out to get you or you are never good enough to end the cycle. Many times, it comes back to the simple phrase of letting go and letting God. Too many of us want to lay our burdens at the foot of the cross, but due to our desire to be perfect and inpatients, we will lay it down and pick it right back up because we want it fixed, and we want it fixed now. This only leads to further destruction to relationships, situations, and circumstances.

The current trauma cycle that has been occurring within my family since I was small is still ongoing. Trying to heal while on the cycle is next to impossible. Understanding and forgiveness is so important but also owning your own mistakes. I know that through my grief, pain, frustration, and anger, I could be hurtful as a child, teen, and daughter; however, I was never having anyone jumping in, trying to provide me the mental help or capacity that I needed to get through my emotions. I see now that my contribution to the emotional roller coaster with my mother was a double-edged sword, although now it seems that I am one of the few within the family that will identify that the trauma cycle needs to end. The remainder members see it but feel that it is not their place to take a stand. Their thought process is just let it be. My mother is how she is. Ignore it and do what you want to do, but in my eyes, that only feeds the beast when I or anyone else stands against it, making it so difficult to get out of the trauma cycle, heal, or stop the trauma cycle altogether. In times like this, it is important to seek out the Lord and wait on Him and His directions.

> For I know the plans I have for you, declares the Lord, plans for welfare and not for evil, to give you a future and a hope. Then you will call upon me and come and pray to me, and I will hear you. You will seek me and find me when you seek me with your whole heart. I will be found by you, declares the Lord and I will restore your fortunes and gather your from all the nations and all the places where I have driven you, declares the Lord, and I will bring you back to the place from where I sent you into exile. (Jeremiah 29:11–14 ESV)

It has been these verses that have brought me to where I am today. These places that we have been sent may have been through the will of God or we may have sent ourselves there based on our own plans and not God's plan, while He allowed our faith to be tried and tested our faith so that we would return to Him, seeking Him and His wisdom, strength, grace, power, mercy, and forgiveness. I do believe that, at times, we tend to exile ourselves away from God because of how we feel so unworthy. But the key we must remember is we are promised many things in these few verses.

1. God promises that our future plans are plans of hope and prosperous.
2. God will hear us.
3. We will find God when we seek Him with our whole heart.
4. God will restore us and our fortunes.
5. He will bring us back out of our exiles, whether it be from Him or ourselves.

Therefore, with the relationship with my mother, I will not seek answers within my own wisdom. I will seek answers through and by God, for my hope of a wonderful and peaceful future.

FIGHTING DEMONS WHILE CHASING GOD!

I feel that God has provided answers over the last year, with that of forgiveness and accepting his healing. Many people may think that by stepping back and taking a long break in the relationship with my mother, that forgiveness has not occurred. But in reality, it has. However, I can continue subjecting myself to appropriate, uncalled-for behaviors because it only brings out the evil of my flesh, making the healing process not happen. I often think of the scripture where Christ tells the disciples to forgive seventy times seven; many, it needs to be endless forgiveness because God does that for us. Although I believe God only forgives when you have true remorse and a change in behavior. I have truly forgiven my mother, but until there is a change in behavior, I do not want to stumble and fall short in my obedience to the Lord. Learning that in all relationships even the one you have with the Lord, the condition of your heart matters. True salvation only comes when there is accountability for your behaviors, repentance, and a change in your heart. This is true with your relationship with others as well. Unless every individual is willing to change the traumatizing behaviors, then the relationship becomes toxic, allowing open doors for the enemy, Satan, and his demons to enter and create chaos and sin within the lives of the toxic relationship. All that I want is healing for both myself and my mother. All these years that I have been courageous and stood my ground to point out behaviors that are not appropriate, I realize now that it is no longer my place to help my mother heal. I have to turn it over to God and allow him the great healer touch and heal her. I also have to be obedient and cling to God by allowing him to heal me. The key is finding peace in the Lord and gratitude for all the blessings he has bestowed even in the trials. I am now focusing on building my faith in the Lord, and he will heal hearts and relationships where I could not.

Consider it all joy, my brethren, when you encounter various trials, knowing that the testing of your faith produces endurance. (James 1:2–3 ESV)

CHAPTER 7

Being Restored

Praise the Lord, all nations! Extol him, all peoples! For great is his steadfast love toward us, and the faithfulness of the Lord endures forever. Praise the Lord.

—Psalm 117 (ESV)

This is the day that the Lord has made;
let us rejoice and be glad in it.

—Psalm 118:24 (ESV)

The Lord certainly knew what wonderful plans that He had for me and my future. It had been a few weeks after Derrick died, and my future husband stepped into my life. I had finally hit the level of maturity that God felt I was ready for the next step. I just didn't feel ready myself.

I had been in such a depressed state that I finally had a long conversation with God and told him that I could not take the pain anymore and begged him to heal my heart. My heart is still on the mend, but he healed the portion that had been broken by Derrick's death. One of the fellows that I had dated whom I thought was a jerk just so happened he just needed to grow up too. That fellow's name was Robby, and he attended the same church I did. Robby approached me about three weeks after Derrick died and talked a bit, offering his apologies and told me if I ever wanted to get out of the house or get some ice cream, then just give him a call, and we would go. Well, I smiled politely and thanked him for the offer, but after I walked away, I was like, never in this lifetime. He had hurt me once, and I had just had the most painful experience in my life. I was determined that it was not going to happen again. It is funny, you might say that, but God had different plans.

Two months later, he asked me if he could come over and watch a movie with me, and I was like, okay, not thinking it would lead to anywhere, and not twenty-five years later, we have been happily married for twenty-four of those years, had four beautiful children and a wonderful home together. Don't get me wrong. We have had our ups and downs as any normal married couple would have; however, we have worked through them with the help of the Lord. God is at the center of our relationship, and it has been important to both of us that we have sought to put Him in the center of our relationship. God taught me with Derrick of what it felt like to be loved, like I had always wanted, but He brought me true unconditional love with Robby. God brought the nurturing that I had always needed from a man, through Robby. He brought me a best friend through thick or thin. He brought me someone that would hold me accountable when I was being unreasonable or irrational, and He brought me my biggest defender with Robby.

Witnessing the love that Robby bestows on me and my children has been a lifelong dream. Through my discussions with Caroline and the insight to look for God in everything, I realized that I was finally getting the family I always wanted and felt that I deserved. What I find so amazing is God blessed me and has continually fulfilled His promises to me. I am so humbled and filled with gratitude that it sometimes can be so overwhelming of how grateful I am to the future plans God has provided me. I look back at that lost, hurt, and pain-stricken sixteen-year-old, feeling hopeless, given just a few simple words of "God has a plan for your life" that I would never have imagined it to be so grand. God is good all the time, and all the time, God is good.

Don't think that oh well, now I am living a trial-free, obstacle-free, or demon-free life. Oh no! Those demons, trials, and obstacles still show up ready and waiting to pounce and attack me. Remember, God has a purpose for me. Those seeds of faith over the years, applying scripture, deepening my relationship with the Lord, drawing closer to Him, don't think that I haven't hit some hard spells. I have. However, all the years that I felt as if I was facing those trials alone, Caroline has helped me understand that I was facing them with God. Now, even better, I am facing them with God and my family that He has provided me.

I started working in the youth ministry at our church as well as teaching Sunday school classes. I started a young girls' group called Girls of Faith, and we would meet and interact on missions together. I was living my best life, serving and honoring the Lord.

I had always wanted to work in the medical field, even thinking that I would like to be a doctor of some sort. However, falling in love and having children rearranged those plans for me. I was a certified medical assistant for six years, and then I stayed at home for a bit because I was working to pay someone else to raise my children whom I wanted to raise. Unfortunately, Caroline explained that due to being by myself during my childhood, it could have brought back traumatic references for me, making it very hard on me mentally to be at home. Once I had my fourth child, the disarray of my hormones and the depression setting in from my childhood trauma, I couldn't take it, and I had to start working part-time at least. It was a time in my life when my vulnerabilities were arising and the enemy was taking advantage of it. All the emotions that God had begun to heal were flooding back because I had become lukewarm with God. I became a long-term substitute teacher at the local elementary school that my two oldest children went to. I absolutely fell in love with teaching. Fortunately, Pfeiffer University was at that time sending some of its professors to Randolph Community College to allow those with associate degrees to finish their bachelor's degrees out in elementary education. So I went back to school so that I could help provide for our family.

FIGHTING DEMONS WHILE CHASING GOD!

During these early years, I was not a great mother. The demons that had influenced my childhood and brought about those traumatic experiences had started to embed themselves in my life, and I was turning into that searching person, trying to fill the empty void. When in reality, I had all I needed with the Lord and my family. I tried so hard to be a better mother figure than what I had experienced; but, unfortunately, when the stress got the best of me, I would use the same degrading and belittling words that I had heard, which damaged a bit of my relationships with my older children. That is why this past Christmas, we finally had a sit-down, and they told me everything so that I could ask for their forgiveness and change to improve our relationships because I didn't want my children to have the same relationship with me as I still have with my mother, touch and go, not very close.

When I began teaching full-time, it was at a small Christian school in Troy. I remember, one day, in chapel, I could feel God calling me to the mission field, but I never quite understood. I thought the children of WesCare was my mission field. I continued to work and share the Gospel; however, I began to get more challenges, trials, and obstacles. Sometimes these trials were with my kids or my marriage or work. It seemed as if the enemy was constantly pushing back against anything that I would try to do and move forward in the Lord.

As my children got older and were wanting to be involved in sports, and the leadership of the school was starting to decline, it felt as if it was time to move on. It just so happened that right at the end, I received a terrible injury. I was playing basketball with the students, and I got hit and knocked to the floor and received a terrible concussion. It took a while, but I finally slowly healed from that injury. We changed schools, and I began teaching at Fayetteville Street Christian School. The children went there with me as well so that they could play sports.

It was a great few years, and my faith and knowledge of what God had for me was growing so much. I felt as if I was fulfilling my purpose in serving the Lord while also gaining enjoyment and fulfillment from my role as a teacher. I was able to share my story and the Gospel with the students, helping them with their struggles and seeking out their faith and their own relationships with the Lord. However, my health began to fade. I was getting worse and worse, while not getting any information from doctors. I began falling, passing out, becoming so weak I could not move. The brain fog and lack of focus was killing me. But I was not going to allow my health to deter me from my mission of serving the Lord. Looking back now, it is almost amusing at what the enemy was trying to do at the time, and I could not see it. I still had not got to the full understanding of what God wanted from me and my life. I hadn't completely understood my calling or at least my calling at that point. I thought that God was using me at the school to help influence and bring to light some inconsistencies.

By the third year at the school, a new administrator had come in, and he and I did not see eye to eye on the importance of ministering to the students. The current administrator desired to focus on the outward appearance of students more so than building relationships with them and getting them to understand the sinful condition of their hearts. I, however, viewed things quite the opposite. I was not more worried about their hem lines, hair, and clothing as much as I was worried about the sinful nature of their hearts. He felt that he had to clean the outside of the vessel with legalistic issues of clothing, etc., more so than the condition of the heart of the child. I, however, saw it the opposite. You must seek to help the condition of the heart of the children before demanding legalistic issues of clothing, etc. on the children. Due to that, and my health continually declining, I decided to leave in the middle of the year and focus on my health and getting better for my family.

> While Jesus was speaking a Pharisee asked him to dine with him, so he went and reclined at the table. The Pharisee was astonished to see that he did not first wash before dinner. And the Lord said to him, "Now you Pharisees cleanse the outside of the cup and dish, but inside you are full of greed and wickedness! You fools! Did not he that

> made the outside make the inside also? But give as alms those things that are within, and behold, everything is clean for you." (Luke 11:37–40 ESV)

I have often found that when I tend to follow my own direction more than I am following God's will for my life, He tends to bring me back in a place where I can truly focus on Him. With my unknown illness getting worse, and the frustration that it was getting harder and harder to care for myself and my family, I became angry and resentful toward God. I had many conversations with God in the shower, driving down the road, and begged for answers and what He wanted from me and from my life. I had been broken mentally, physically, emotionally, and now spiritually that I had no idea what He was wanting from me and my life as a child of God. What I didn't realize was that maybe it was some of my own sin and arrogance that had gotten me to the point of frustration and waywardness from the Lord and His plan for my life. How often we want to blame others for our sin, including God. I feel that many of my latest trials have been for me to learn how to fight for the Lord and what is morally right and how to own my own mistakes and sins.

> Behold, I am sending you out as sheep in the midst of wolves, so be wise as servants and innocent as doves. Beware of men, for that will deliver you over to the courts and flog you in their synagogues, and you will be dragged before governors and kings for my sake to bear witness before them and the Gentiles. (Matthew 10:16–18 ESV)

How often have we been faced with circumstances or situations, and we have sought out the wisdom of the Lord or allowed the Holy Spirit to speak through us? We all have been given special talents and a specific purpose. God knew and had written all of our days before there were any. The questions I have been asking myself were when are you going to start fully living for God and stop being lukewarm?

> *So because you are lukewarm, and neither hot nor cold, I will spit you out of my mouth. (Revelation 3:16 ESV)*

CHAPTER 8

Journey Forward

> And he said to them, "Go into all the world and proclaim the gospel to the whole creation. Whoever believes and is baptized will be saved, but whoever does not believe will be condemned."
>
> —Mark 16:15–16 (ESV)

My journey from this point is to run the race of sharing the Gospel with others. With the encouragement of Caroline, I feel that God has given me my journey to share the saving grace and salvation that I have found in my Lord Jesus Christ, along with the restoration of my brokenness to others that could be experiencing similar demons. I know, on more than one occasion, the spiritual battles that turn into emotional, physical, and personal battles can alter our perspectives of God and His love and grace. I fall short every day and fight to get back on the next day that God allows me to be here.

My heart for the unbelievers, unknowing, and children that are being suppressed by the evils of society. It is the desire of my heart to share the gospel in a way that others can see that there is hope for the future through Christ Jesus. The promises of God are true. My current frustration with myself is, why have I waited so long to answer the calling of the Lord? Why does anyone wait? Life challenges and circumstances often become our excuses, but that is just it, they are excuses. Our very breath that we are taking is by the love and grace of God. Why are we waiting on sharing what He is doing in our lives? I know that God opens doors.

I am once again back at home being re-centered on God's will for my life. I had finally reached a full circle. I had gone back to the first small Christian school I taught at to become the principal. God called me there for a reason; however, the enemy had other plans, and the mission I felt God had called me to was very quickly unraveling. I didn't understand. I was hurt that people of God could act in such un-Christlike ways. Then I remembered, even those closest to God are not off limits for the enemy to destroy the spreading of the Gospel. We all fall victim to sins of pride, jealousy, envy, and fear. I know that I have fell to these sins in particular, many times, but that is where forgiveness, mercy, grace, and humility should make its way into our lives, and we should love each other enough to see us through our sin as God sees us. Unfortunately, that sin nature of the flesh begins to attack and overcome and blinds us to the ultimate goal of the Lord, and that is sharing the Gospel, going out, making disciples, growing the kingdom of God.

We often, as church members, get set in our ways of growing within the four walls of the physical building and forget that the church is the group of believers, not a physical structure. We as Christian have got to change our mindset to a growth mindset of kingdom growth and not growth within the physical structure. Why are we not sharing what God is doing in our lives on social media, in our neighborhoods, among our family members? What is holding us back from sharing the incredible sunrise or sunset God has allowed us to witness, yet again, another day, a day that He provided for us to interact with someone and share the Gospel? When was the last time you shared a piece of your story and became vulnerable to a stranger so that the Holy Spirit could speak through you? Scripture tells us not to be anxious, that the Holy Spirit will speak through us.

> When they deliver you over do not be anxious how you are to speak or what you are to say, for what you are to say will be given to you in that

> hour. For it is not you who speak, but the Spirit of your Father speaking through you. (Matthew 10:19–20 ESV)

I know for certain that this book will rock the boat, but one thing that I have learned through my various trials in the last two years is that I am a boat-rocker. If we as Christians do not become more vocal and more of a contender for the enemy, we will all be devoured.

Something so precious to me as a school administrator is watching the innocence of the children and how their love and burden for the Lord became so evident and real. My favorite thing to see was watching them sing, "My God is so big, my God is so mighty, there is nothing my God cannot do." Another favorite song of the students was "Waymaker." Man, it tore me up to see those precious children get so invested in that song that it reminded me of my true calling and that was to share the Gospel, whether it be through speaking, teaching, leading, or even writing that was what I was to do. That is why as I am wrapping up this first book (yes, God has already laid others on my heart to write). I am sitting on my front porch, filled, bursting forth with such gratitude in His authority and guidance. I know I'm going to be heading into a battle, but like the song goes, "My God is so big, my God is so mighty, there is nothing my God cannot do."

I hope that you were able to glean a fraction of the love, grace, and mercy that I have obtained from God my Savior. I hope, by the time you have finished this book, if you do not know Jesus Christ as your Savior, you use your Bible and seek Him with your whole heart and He will guide you through to find your salvation in Him. Remember, it is simply recognizing you are a sinner as we all are, and that the only way to be redeemed is to trust, believe with your whole heart that Jesus Christ lived, ministered, died, and rose again on the third day so that He could take on all the sin—past, present, and future—for all of mankind to have the opportunity to have salvation and conquer the grave. It is a complete heart transformation, and with the true heart transformation, the rest of you will continue to grow and change, becoming more and more like Christ.

Allow me to say this final prayer with you, my precious friend and reader: Dear heavenly Father, You are so precious and Holy that we praise Your name for bringing us together in this book. We thank You for the healing process this has had for me and the opportunity to share the Gospel with my friend. I pray that if those that are reading this now do not know You as their Savior they come to the knowledge through this testimony. If perhaps my friend reading this has moved away from Your truth and Word, and this testimony has brought them back to a point of reconciliation, I pray that You will have your blessing on them. I pray for the upcoming battles that I know, without a doubt, the enemy is planning, and I pray that You go ahead of me and protect me and my friends reading this from all evil the enemy is planning. Dear precious Lord, thank You, most of all, for Your Son, Jesus Christ, and the sacrifice He made for mankind on the cross. Lord, we are humbled at Your majestic work of creation and pray that You continue to provide us days that we may share our story of salvation, grace, mercy, and forgiveness with others so they might be able to come to you. In Christ Jesus, we pray. And everyone say, "*Amen!*"

> *Have I not commanded you? Be Strong and Courageous! Do not be frightened, and do not be dismayed, for the Lord your God is with you where ever you go. (Joshua 1:9 ESV)*

ABOUT THE AUTHOR

Kimberly Faith Cagle is a new and upcoming Christian author, with the desire to honor and bring glory to her Lord and Savior, Jesus Christ. She has been in the education field for fifteen years and is a doctoral candidate in educational leadership from Liberty University. She has been very happily married to her husband for twenty-four years, and they have four beautiful children. As Faith has been tirelessly seeking to serve the Lord, she has not been without battles. It is those battles that has strengthened her faith in God that she has taken a leap of faith and began pursuing a career in Christian writing and ministry. Her hope is to minister in the form of writing and public speaking on behalf of her heavenly Father, while helping others in their walk with Christ.

Printed in the USA
CPSIA information can be obtained
at www.ICGtesting.com
LVHW091508170924
791302LV00002B/183

9 798890 433183